THE SAINT WITHIN

TWELVE STRATEGIES TO STRENGTHEN YOUR INNER YOGĪ

KALAKAṆṬHA DASA

The Saint Within - Twelve Strategies to Strengthen Your Inner Yogī

Kalakaṇṭha Dasa (Carl Woodham)
carlwoodham@gmail.com

Published by Sweetsong Publications
ISBN-13: 9781092681933

Design & Layout by:
HoofprintMedia.com

THE SAINT WITHIN

TWELVE STRATEGIES TO STRENGTHEN YOUR INNER YOGĪ

KALAKAṆṬHA DASA

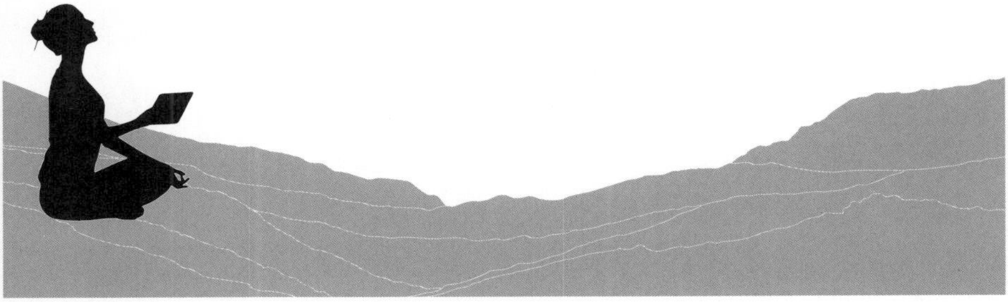

CONTENTS

Foreword 7
Introduction & Notes 9

1: Sūta. Practice Bhakti Yoga 17

2: Nārada. Ask a Guru 29

3: Draupadī. Act with Compassion 41

4: Kuntī. Set Spiritual Priorities 53

5: Bhīṣma. Cultivate the Mode of Goodness 63

6: Bhaktas. Serve Without Stipulation 77

7: Yudhiṣṭhir. Look Ahead 87

8: Dhṛtarāstra. Get Real 93

9: Arjuna. Think of Krishna 103

10: Dharma. Forgive 117

11: Viṣnurāta. Let Go 131

12: Śukadeva. Take Action 145

Afterword 159
Key Personalities 160
Glossary 165
Acknowledgements 168

THE SAINT WITHIN

TWELVE STRATEGIES TO STRENGTHEN YOUR INNER YOGĪ

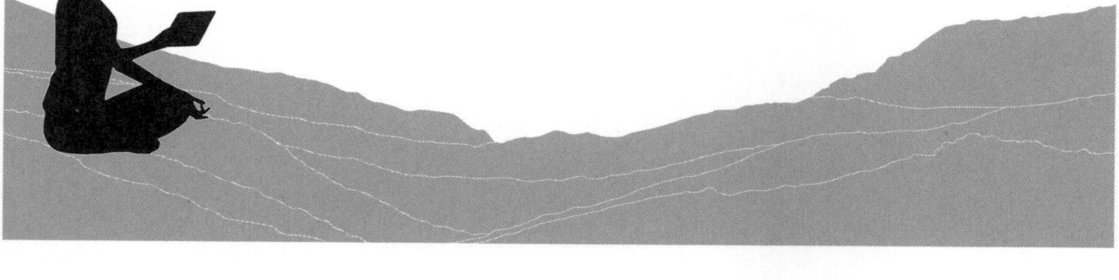

FOREWORD

In my childhood, as my grandmother put me to sleep each night, she would tell and retell stories from the *Bhāgavat Purāṇa*. Though I thoroughly enjoyed the stories of Prahlāda, Dhruva, and Kṛishna, I always wondered how it all began. Who wrote the *Bhāgavat*? Who first told these stories? Years later I learned the answers from a multi-volume prose English translation that my grandfather gave to me.

The Saint Within helps join these dots too, but in a brilliantly poetic way that offers the English reader some of the sweetness, rhyme, and rhythm experienced in original Sanskrit language. Despite its deep philosophy, the *Bhāgavat* is essentially poetry, and its passion and drama can easily be lost in pedantic prose translations. In the past I assumed that the subtleties of poetic meter and the sweetness of the Sanskrit rhythm would never be accessible to English-speaking audiences. *The Saint Within* has challenged my assumptions by making me feel the poetry of the Bhāgavat despite the constraints and cultural differences of English.

Further, as traditional commentaries on the *Bhāgavat* deepen an appreciation of the text itself, so has this rendition of the *Bhāgavat*. Successful commentators embellish sacred texts by understanding and applying them personally, then making them relevant to others. Thus, the best translations of texts such as this convey their messages as lived values. Let me tell you a story about that.

Five hundred years ago, the saint and spiritual reformer Sri Caitanya Mahāprabhu loved the *Bhāgavat* with all his heart and lived its message in his life. Once, while traveling to share the *Bhāgavat*'s message, he met Raghunātha Paṇḍita, who lived on the bank of the Ganges in the village of Barāhanagar, about three miles north of present-day Calcutta.

Raghunātha, a poet-scholar, understood and explained the *Bhāgavat* masterfully, causing Caitanya to swoon in mystical ecstasy with his narrations. Caitanya later requested the pundit to render the entire *Bhāgavat* into Bengali, so audiences who didn't know Sanskrit could savor its deep philosophy and poetic feeling. Thus, Raghunātha Paṇdit crafted a beautiful book called *Kṛṣṇa-prema-taraṅginī,* or Love-streams for Kṛishna, that Caitanya relished, as have his Bengali-reading followers ever since. And true to the tradition, their lives exemplified the text they read and rendered to their audiences.

Kalakaṇṭḥa Dasa's *The Saint Within* continues that tradition of poetically rendering the *Bhāgavat Purāṇa* in regional languages, even one as globalized as English. Dasa's poetry, like that of his medieval predecessor, captures the poetic heart of the original Sanskrit *Bhāgavat*, despite being in a language that is worlds away from the original. After reading *The Saint Within* (as well as his earlier books), I feel that the same energy that manifested *Kṛṣṇa-prema-taraṅginī* is now shaping Kalakaṇṭḥa Dasa's poetry.

The Saint Within continues the legacy of Raghunātha Paṇdita, whom Caitanya called Bhāgavatāchārya, or a great teacher of the Bhāgavat. I hope Kalakaṇṭḥa Dasa is able to finish rendering all of the remaining cantos of the *Bhāgavat* into English poetry, offering to the world a priceless gift as his predecessor Bhāgavatacharya did five hundred years back.

Meanwhile, with this masterful English poetic version of the first and second of the *Bhāgavat*'s twelve cantos in hand, I wish you happy reading.

Dr. Abhi Ghosh
Faculty of Religious Studies
Grand Valley State University
Michigan, USA.

INTRODUCTION

We are not human beings having a spiritual experience. We are spiritual beings having a human experience.

Pierre Teilhard de Chardin

In the course of yoga practice, a serious yogi gradually comes to identify with his or her body's living force instead of the body itself. Then, through meditation and study, the yogi learns to stretch, stimulate and strengthen the inner self. Whether knowing it or not, at that point the yogi is on the path to saintliness. What happens next?

A man once met an old college friend at a restaurant. "Remember Johnson?" said the friend. "He's a Federal judge."

"Johnson a Federal judge?" said the man. "Impossible!"

"No, it's true. I saw him in his robes."

"Well, maybe," grumbled the man, "but he can't be getting a Federal judge's salary."

So it is with saintliness. Even if someone appears saintly, are they really endowed with spiritual ecstasy 24/7 or just going through the motions?

The yoga system focused on inner development is known as bhakti-yoga. When we independently discovered bhakti in our late teens, my wife and I had no aspiration for saintliness. Still, ten years later, when we met and married, we continued our bhakti-yoga practices together as we raised three children and ran a real estate business. Though we never felt particularly saintly, through bhakti, as learned from our teacher, Śrila Prabhupada, we learned to treasure a simple external life endowed with rich inner experiences. When we retired in 2006, we opened the Bhakti Academy in Gainesville, Florida. Since then we have shared the pleasantly surprising joys of bhakti-yoga with thousands of students.

This book aims to help yogīs everywhere looking for inner enlightenment and strength to realize, through bhakti, that some degree of saintliness resides within us all.

Every spiritual tradition has its saints. In addition to those beatified by the Catholic Church, there are the Jewish *tzadik*, the Islamic *walī*, the Hindu *rishi*, the Sikh guru, and the Buddhist *bodhisattva*. Then there are everyday people who walk amongst us who may also justifiably be called saints. So, what makes someone a saint? Some traits immediately come to mind: a saint would be peaceful, honest, compassionate, wise, patient, tolerant, and forgiving. How many people fit this description? Sadly, not many. Yet India's ancient Vedic wisdom insists that saintliness is a natural state of being for any well-rounded person.

Some may rightfully ask, "What value is saintliness when being pushy, dishonest, and heartless gets you to the top? If good things come to good people, why do selfish materialists so often seem more successful?"

Simply put, actual success eludes such people. More than merely being on top materially, success means being happy. Materialists look outside of themselves for happiness and find only petty, fleeting pleasures, whereas true saints know how to find deep, lasting happiness within. If we want to tap in to real happiness, we need to find our saint within.

Uncovering saintliness takes more than developing noble qualities. It presupposes a belief in, or at least an open mind to, the existence of a Supreme Being. Dear reader, if you feel that there is no Supreme, an ordinary self-improvement book might work better for you. The bhakti approach is different: sustainable self-improvement comes naturally when one connects with the Person who is the source and the epitome of all saintly qualities. That Person is the Supreme. We may refer to Him as Jehovah, Allah, or, as herein, as Krishna. The connection is important, not the nomenclature.

YOGA AS UNION WITH THE SUPREME

Connecting with the Supreme Person is called yoga, a series of steps beginning with physical exercise and ending in sainthood. As physical (*haṭha*) yoga exercises bring strength, stamina, flexibility and a sense of well-being to our bodies, yoga in its deeper sense does the same for our inner selves. This deeper yoga practice is known as bhakti. The *Bhagavad-gītā*, the classic yoga textbook, defines bhakti as the ultimate goal of all yoga.

Text 2.70 of the *Bhagavad-gītā* describes how bhakti changes our inner life:

> A person who is undisturbed by the incessant flow of desires that enter like rivers into the ocean which is ever being filled but always still, can alone achieve peace, not one who strives to satisfy such desires.

By seeing through the trap of material desire, bhakti-yogīs, or bhaktas, gain self-control and experience tranquility in any circumstance. To be undisturbed in turbulent times, to be satisfied with simple things, to tap in to a boundless source of inner joy, to act thoughtfully, to treat others kindly and fairly, to enjoy constant peace of mind—these are the fruits of inner yoga savored by successful, inwardly fit bhaktas.

FAQS

Q: If we focus on the inner self, what becomes of our outer self?

A: That's also addressed. Better self-discipline leads the bhakta to stick to a healthy diet and exercise regime so the material body is maintained at optimal fitness. The inner yogī nourishes and strengthens the outer yogī as well.

Q: What is inner fitness?

A: The bhakta's inner yogī becomes well-toned, bringing deep satisfaction with life and reduced dependence on ever-changing externals. Bhaktas become free of ulterior motives and can get along with nearly anyone. They navigate setbacks well and avoid pride by attributing their successes to the Supreme. Free of defensiveness and ego, bhaktas express themselves thoughtfully and creatively. This increased enjoyment of life gradually evolves into a powerful sense of love for the Supreme, an ecstasy that fully enlivens and uplifts the bhakta even as he or she moves to their final breath.

Q: Couldn't one achieve all this without having any connection with the Supreme? Why is having a loving relationship with the Supreme Person a prerequisite for saintliness?

A: Love is the most powerful way of connecting with anyone. Directing our loving propensity to the Supreme Person through bhakti connects us with the source of all saintly qualities. It's like connecting a pipeline to an unlimited reservoir, allowing saintliness to flow through us. This results in astonishing improvement in our character and quality of life.

Q: Does redirecting our love to the Supreme through bhakti-yoga diminish our love for others, such as family, friends and pets?

A: No, quite the opposite: loving the Supreme expands our ability to love everyone. Saints see all souls as dear to the Supreme Person and, hence, dear to them, for "A friend of yours is a friend of mine." At the same time, from the solid position of loving the imperishable, bhaktas keep their perishable relationships in perspective. While bhaktas naturally increase their love for family and friends, they also better endure the inevitable end of these external relationships. Such is the bhakti path to sainthood.

THE SCIENCE OF BHAKTI

Bhakti applies in any spiritual tradition. As with all yoga, it is a systematic practice that does not demand commitment to dogma or a conversion experience. All that's required is an open mind to objectively experiment with the process and then judge by the results.

Though all spiritual texts contain hints of bhakti, the ancient Sanskrit classic *Bhāgavat Purāṇa*, known as the postgraduate study of *Bhagavad-gītā*, has bhakti as its exclusive focus. The *Bhāgavat Purāṇa* teaches bhakti both philosophically and practically.

The *Bhāgavat Purāṇa* contains fascinating narrations of incidents from the lives of renowned bhaktas past. Just learning about these exemplary bhaktas helps us strengthen our own inner yogī. These renowned personalities undergo loss, angst, depression, fear—the full range of human experience—in trying, even superhuman circumstances. Seeing how they respond to challenges with connection to the Supreme reveals new options in our own lives.

The *Bhāgavat Purāṇa* was originally composed in exquisite Sanskrit verse and meter. Reading it daily for nearly fifty years has enriched my life with the beauty of the language and the joy of bhakti. To capture for the English reader both the poetic form and the spirit of the original Sanskrit composition, I have rendered the English translations of its introductory chapters in to poetic verse. Each of the twelve sections of this edition focuses on a different saint from the pages of the *Bhāgavat Purāṇa* and gleans strategies from their experiences that will help us progress on our own paths to sainthood.

One of the saintly strategies missing from these twelve is, "Be humble." That's because practicing bhakti automatically puts one in a humble position. Bhakti means loving service to the Supreme, a goal that is completely opposite of trying to become one with the Supreme through yoga or mediation. A good servant is naturally humble, and a good master naturally reciprocates lovingly with his sincere and attentive servant. The more the servant wants to please the master, the more the master wants to please the servant. The *Bhagavad-gita* thus describes bhakti as *nitya-yuktā-upāsate*, an endless, ever-deepening loving exchange between the yogi and the Supreme.

Reading the *Bhāgavat Purāṇa* is itself one of the potent methods of bhakti. Even a newcomer can quickly experience its sustainable, life-changing effects. As described in a memorable couplet found early in the text:

> By reading the *Bhāgavat Purāṇa* and by directing service to the Supreme, all that is troublesome to the heart is almost completely destroyed and loving service to the Supreme becomes irrevocably established.[1]

In other words, just by reading a little from this book each day, bad habits will lose their grip and saintly qualities will appear in your life as if from nowhere, along with cascades of inner happiness. Bhakti will give you a taste of spiritual bliss that makes all mundane pleasures pale in comparison. It will allow you to see so clearly how materialistic life represses your inner saint that you will spontaneously reorganize both your inner and outer life for the better.

Open the door of your mind through bhakti and let your true self, your inner saint, come out into the sunlight.

Kalakaṇṭḥa das

[1] *Bhagavāt Purāna* 1.2.18

NOTES ON THIS TRANSLATION

Chapters One through Eleven of *The Saint Within* include poetic renditions of nearly all of the roughly 1000 original Sanskrit texts found in the First Canto of the *Bhāgavat Purāṇa*. Chapter Twelve consists of selected verses from the much shorter Second Canto.

In the poetic sections, Vyās, the author and omniscient narrator of the *Bhāgavat Purāṇa*, introduces the book and, in places, writes about himself in the third person. Vyās's statements are always shown in italics.

Vyās describes a gathering of sages in which Sūta answers spiritual questions. Sūta is the functional narrator of the *Bhāgavat Purāṇa*, so his statements appear without quotation marks. Quotation marks appear only when Sūta or Vyās are quoting other speakers.

Some Sanskrit names and terms are used in this book. If you're new to them, here are some partial guidelines to help you pronounce them with some accuracy:

The a is pronounced as the u in but.
The ā is pronounced as the a in far.
The e is pronounced as the a in navy.
The i is pronounced as the i in pin.
The ī is pronounced as the i in pique.
The ṛ is a vowel pronounced like the ri in rim.
The ś or ṣ are pronounced (roughly) as the sh in shore.

The texts presented herein are primarily extracted from Srila A.C. Bhaktivedanta Swami Prabhupada's classic *Śrimad Bhāgavatam*. They are supplemented with occasional inclusions from Śrila Prabhupāda's various commentaries, as well as sections of the *Mahābhārata*. ***Kd***

ONE

SŪTA

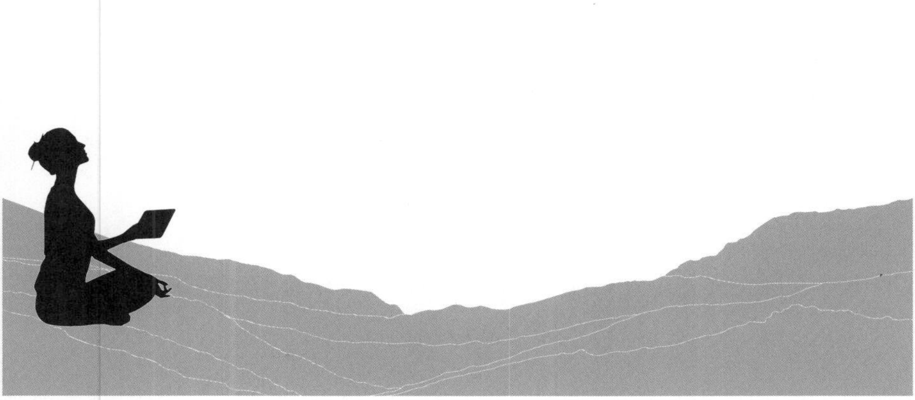

INVOCATION: KRISHNA AND THE *BHĀGAVAT PURĀṆA* (1-6)

I bow to Krishna, Lord of all, the greatest Personality.

Lord Krishna, all the universes rise at Your decree,
and You maintain, destroy and recreate them endlessly.
Lord Krishna, You cause everything, though no one causes You,
and You know every atom that You vanquish and renew.

You organized the Vedic hymns for all to understand
then sung them to Brahmā within his heart as time began.
You engineered a world of matter, tricking all to chase
mirages of enjoyment that dry up without a trace.

Combining goodness, dark and passion with such matchless flair,
You make this world appear important, though it's wisps of air.
I contemplate Lord Krishna, self-contained in His abode,
forever free of falseness and the stain of nature's modes.

Rejecting all pretentious prayers of hidden motivation,
this sacred text addresses those of worthy inclination.
By separating truth from lies as sharply as a knife,
the Bhāgavat *uproots the reader's miseries in life.*

Assembled by the writer Vyās in his maturity,
the Bhāgavat *enlightens one with great efficiency.*
What other scripture anywhere so easily imparts
ecstatic love of God through revelation in the heart?

Oh thoughtful soul, enjoy this book, the Vedas' ripened fruit.
Already sweet to those engaged in spiritual pursuit,

the Bhāgavat *grows sweeter when the son of Vyās repeats*
his father's words, as parrots sweeten mangos with their beaks.

THE SAGES QUESTION SŪTA (7-18)

Within a sacred forest glen five thousand years ago,
the fires of many sages set the early dawn aglow.
While planning lengthy sacrifices, all the sages feared
their nemesis, the dreaded age of Kali, had appeared.

In need of able leadership, the learned sages deemed
the sage Sūta Goswāmī, of them all, was most esteemed.
Withholding urgent questions that the circumstances raised,
the sages spoke to Sūta with these pleasant words of praise:

"Because you are so learned and your life is free of vice,
to hear from you encompasses the perfect sacrifice.
Dear sir, you've learned the scriptures and the ancient histories
by hearing them submissively from great authorities.

You know what Vyās and other learned teachers in his line
intended us to understand at this decisive time.
Because you served them modestly, your gurus favored you,
and we feel very certain you can tell us what to do.

Dear Sūta, with your wisdom, kindly help us ascertain
the highest truth and knowledge as the ancients have explained.
Present to us in words that can be plainly understood
the truth that will bring people absolute and final good.

For in this evil age of Kali, people's lives are brief.
Distressed and lost, they loiter, fight and fret without relief.
So please appraise the scriptures and select essential parts,
the finest sacred teachings to uplift the human heart.

You understand why Krishna, son of Devakī, appears,
so kindly speak about Him for our eager, waiting ears.
Describe to us His many incarnations, each in turn,
for hearing and discussing them is good for all concerned.

Lord Krishna's holy name, though said but once with random breath,
can frighten fear itself and free the soul from birth and death.
To sanctify by Gaṇgā bath takes many, many tries,
but simple talk of Krishna's pastimes quickly purifies.

What person wanting freedom from this dreadful Kali age
would miss the chance to listen to a Krishna conscious sage?
Since learned souls like you can see Lord Krishna's deeds and grace,
please tell us how He manifests to suit each time and place.

The topics of Lord Krishna are transcendent and sublime,
and those with taste for Krishna love to hear them all the time.
With elder brother Balarām and costumed as a man,
Lord Krishna rendered wondrous deeds. What was His master plan?

Quite soon this age of Kali shall destroy society,
so kindly speak of Krishna, which itself is piety.
As Providence has sent you, be the captain of our ship
and sail us through this sea of faults, past Kali's fearsome grip.

Dear Sūta, Lord Śrī Krishna, author of the Vedic codes,
has left our mortal planet for His own sublime abode.

Now who will safeguard higher truths? Will wisdom persevere?
Or will religious principles completely disappear?"

THE SCIENCE OF BHAKTI YOGA (19-38)

Wise Sūta thanked the sages for their questions with these words:
Whatever I say henceforward is simply what I heard
from Śukadev Goswāmī, everybody's inspiration.
I'll speak about him often in the course of this narration.

When young and realized Śukadev gave up his family ties,
his learned father Vyās chased after him with plaintive cries.
But only echoes answered as his wise, indifferent son
departed home for good, his training rituals undone.

Now, Vyās condensed the Vedas to concise, instructive codes.
Concerned that they would be misused, he thereafter composed
their author's explanation, the essential Vedic cream,
the *Bhāgavat*, a book by which mankind could be redeemed.

Though Śukadev assimilated *Bhāgavat* at home,
he later spoke its vital words when he was on his own
to help bewildered people struggling in a troubled age.
The *Bhāgavat* thus comes from Śukadev, the foremost sage.
Before reciting *Bhāgavat* and overcoming sin,
I worship Lord Nārāyan and His transcendental twin,
along with Mother Sarasvatī, queen of education,
as well as Śrī Vyās, who first compiled the whole narration.

The questions you have raised are in themselves our very goal.
Such questions deal with Krishna and can satisfy the soul.

The foremost goal that you or any person can obtain
is serving Krishna lovingly, as I shall now explain.
This service must be selfless and continue constantly
to satisfy a seeking soul to maximum degree.

When you serve Krishna with devotion, He at once reveals
the wisdom of detachment from this world and its appeal.
But if you lack the interest to fulfill Lord Krishna's will,
then all your work for money comes eventually to nil.

Finances seems less urgent once your love of God commences.
Lord Krishna's servant uses wealth, but not to serve the senses.
To live to please the senses is both needless and uncouth,
for what's the good of human life if not to learn the truth?

The truth is one, yet understood in three distinctive ways:
great scholars know Brahman, or Krishna's all-pervading rays;
great yogīs know the Supersoul, the Lord who dwells within;
and devotees know Krishna, from whom everything begins.

His service leads to higher truth, devotees realize,
for serving Krishna purely has made them detached and wise.
Whatever mode of life you live, as caste or skills prescribe,
your work becomes perfected when the Lord is satisfied.
So fix your mind on Krishna, Who protects His devotee,
and hear, remember, glorify and serve Him constantly.
On seeing others slice the knot of transient addictions,
what person would not want to hear of Krishna with attention?

To serve the more enlightened souls whose hearts are truly pure
will make your taste to hear of Krishna even more secure.

And as you gain a taste to hear the virtues of the Lord,
Śrī Krishna, in your heart, removes illusion in accord.

A daily class in *Bhāgavat* and service to the pure
will nurse the ailing heart until it grows completely cured.
By simply hearing topics of Lord Krishna every day,
your dormant love for Him will thrive and never go away.

Then service to Lord Krishna, whose descriptions are sublime,
shall root itself within your heart until the end of time.
And once such loving service is established in your heart,
the ill effects of nature's modes diminish and depart.

As lust, desire and greediness are swept out of the way,
you move ahead to goodness and great happiness each day.
In touch with pure devotion and relieved of low desire,
immersed in Krishna science, you'll be thoroughly inspired.
You'll pierce the knot of false attachment, elevate your soul,
and end the chain of karma as your faith takes solid hold.

Throughout the ages, striving transcendentalists delight
in satisfying Krishna as their dormant love ignites.

Such persons serve Lord Krishna in His absolute position
untouched by goodness, dark or passion, nature's three divisions.
As raw wood is surpassed by smoke, and smoke surpassed by fire,
the mode of passion passes dark, while goodness is still higher.
Brahmā, who governs passion, engineers the whole creation,
while Śiva, ruling darkness, brings about its devastation.
And in between, Lord Vishṇu, ruling goodness, oversees.
Lord Vishṇu is Lord Krishna. Serving Him will set you free.

In darkness or in passion one serves ancestors or gods
to build up wealth and dynasty and other worldly frauds.
Though sages hold all others in the highest veneration,
Lord Krishna, not the demigods, receives their adoration.

For Krishna is the certain aim of scriptural decrees,
and Krishna is the goal of Vedic fire, grains and ghee.
Lord Krishna is the purpose of the mystic's meditation,
and ultimately, Krishna is a worker's compensation.
The knowledge of Lord Krishna is the highest to be known.
What penances you practice should be done for Him alone,
for Krishna is religion, now that irreligion's rife.
To say it very simply, Krishna is the goal of life.

KRISHNA IS THE SOURCE OF ALL AVATARS (39-48)

Conceiving this mundane creation, Krishna has designed
both actions and reactions, bouncing back and forth through time.
On seeing people tangled up in karma and travail,
the Lord will often visit, as a king might tour a jail.

Lord Krishna as the Supersoul pervades this world of doom
as blazing fire permeates the wood that it consumes.
The Supersoul is everywhere, although He's only one,
just as a thousand water pots reflect a single sun.
Within the heart of every soul, the Supersoul observes
the soul pursuing matter and the trouble he incurs.

Lord Krishna creates planets full of gods and men and beasts,
and incarnates among them so the good may be released.

These worlds are but a cloud of matter in the spirit sky
created by Lord Vishṇu, where rebellious souls reside.
A parcel of Lord Vishṇu goes within each galaxy,
reclining on a cosmic ocean very comfortably.
A lotus stem appears from Vishṇu's navel as He rests,
from which the cosmic engineer Brahmā then manifests.

The devotees know Vishṇu's sacred resting form becomes
the gateway for Lord Krishna's incarnations, one by one.

Lord Krishna's countless incarnations come eternally,
like rivulets descending from a never-ending sea.
Though all are His expansions, Krishna still remains Supreme,
appearing to end evil and to set His servants free.

And when one tells how Krishna comes in any of these ways,
with heartfelt pure devotion, in the night or in the day,
the constant, bitter suffering we souls have long endured
shall instantly recede before this transcendental cure.

The *Bhāgavat* is also Krishna. Vyās has now revealed
this blissful incarnation in the literary field.
Vyās taught it to Śukadev, and I heard everything
when Śukadev recited it before a dying king.

The *Bhāgavat* is brilliant as the sun that slays the night
that fell upon us all when Krishna left our mortal sight.
Though truth and goodness may have gone with Krishna to His realm,
the *Bhāgavat* lights up the dark; we won't be overwhelmed.

When Śukadev spoke *Bhāgavat*, I gave my rapt attention.
Now I, his servant Sūta, make this faithful repetition.

STRATEGY #1: PRACTICE BHAKTI YOGA

In these powerful introductory words, Sūta teaches the essentials of bhakti. One of the most essential teachings is to respectfully and attentively hear the *Bhāgavat Purāṇa* from a qualified teacher who has heard from a qualified teacher, and on and on. As Krishna says in the *Bhagavada-gītā* (4.2), "The supreme spiritual science must be received through a chain of disciplic succession."

The history of the *Bhāgavat Purāṇa* shows this chain of genuine teachers and disciples. Originally, Lord Krishna Himself spoke it in a nutshell to Brahma, who then passed it on to Nārada. Nārada inspired his disciple, the great sage Vyās, to put it into writing. Vyās, after dedicating his epic to Lord Krishna and all pure-hearted readers, taught it to his son Śukadeva who later became famous for his sweet recitations.[1]

Once, when Śukadeva was repeating his father's book from memory, Sūta Goswami, a great scholar, happened to be present. It is mentioned here that Sūta had humbly served his gurus, and by achieving their favor, he was able to perfectly understand and remember all that Śukadeva had spoken. Later he shared this knowledge with an assembly of sages who were distraught due to Sri Krishna's recent departure from Earth. This recitation of Sūta Goswami comprises the *Bhāgavat Purāṇa* that we have today.

Herein, Sūta assures the assembled sages that through the nonsectarian and scientific process of bhakti yoga, they can remain connected to the supreme person Krishna and achieve all the spiritual benefits of that association. He explains that bhakti—selfless and continual service to the Supreme—brings more joy to life than any other human pursuit. When done correctly, bhakti automatically brings both wisdom and a healthy

---

[1] The name Śukadeva is an indication of this. In Sanskrit, '*śuka*' means parrot. When a parrot pecks a fruit such as a mango, the natural sugars are released and the taste of the fruit is improved.

detachment from this world of pain and pleasure. Through bhakti, anyone can come to understand Krishna, regardless of their education or social status. When one knows the art of bhakti, nearly anything one does can be done for Krishna, turning ordinary tasks into sources of great joy.

Later in the *Bhāgavat Purāṇa*, Suta explains that bhakti has nine methods of practice:

- ***hearing*** about Krishna, such as one does by reading *Bhāgavat Purāṇa*
- ***chanting*** Krishna's names or speaking about Him
- ***remembering*** Krishna, His beautiful form, qualities and activities
- ***serving*** Krishna with devotion
- ***praying*** to Him, for example, for guidance and protection
- ***fulfilling His instructions***, as given in the scriptures and by a qualified teacher
- ***worshipping*** Him, for example, by offering Him food, flowers, and so forth
- ***befriending*** Him – taking Krishna as one's confidential companion
- ***offering all of one's activities*** to Krishna

These processes naturally overlap and enhance each other. For example, hearing or learning about bhakti leads one to try chanting, and that often leads to offering flowers and tasty vegetarian food to Krishna. Wherever there is repetition of the spiritually potent names of Krishna, there will also be hearing and remembering. By serving, praying and worshipping, one's relationship with Krishna grows closer and friendlier up to the point where one falls completely in love with Krishna and wants to do everything for His pleasure.

Out of the nine processes, the Vedic texts recommend the process of chanting the names of the Supreme as most important in the present age (Kali-yuga). Repeating any sacred name softly to oneself constitutes a powerful meditation that is much easier than trying to force the mind into silence. This yogīc practice engages the tongue, the ears and, if done with beads or finger-counting, the sense of touch as well. Where the senses go, the mind tends to follow, so chanting sacred names quickly brings one to a focused meditation on the Supreme. Connecting the soul to the Supreme by chanting His names pleases the heart and pacifies the restless mind.

Some ask, "Why is chanting the names of the Supreme any different from repeating any ordinary word, like Coca-Cola?" If you experiment, you'll find that repeating such mundane sounds quickly grows tiring, while repeating names of the Supreme brings sustainable bliss. Any spiritual name has this effect, be it Buddha, Allah, Jehovah or any of the countless others. Such practice is called mantra meditation. In Sanskrit, "man" means mind and "tra" means to release. Such meditation frees the mind from material entanglement and elevates the chanter to spiritually heightened consciousness.

As there are countless names of the Supreme, there are countless mantras. Bhaktas in the line of the great medieval bhakti teacher Caitanya Mahāprabhu chant the "*maha*" or great mantra: Hare Krishna, Hare Krishna, Krishna Krishna, Hare Hare, Hare Rāma, Hare Rāma, Rāma Rāma, Hare Hare. Rāma and Krishna are names of the Supreme, and Hare invokes Rādhā, the Supreme feminine energy, who is devotion to the Supreme personified. Taken together, the maha-mantra implores the Supreme to engage the chanter in bhakti, or devotional service.

The path of bhakti opens most easily to one who finds camaraderie with fellow seekers of wisdom and truth. In their company one gains a taste for bhakti and discovers the miraculous ways that Krishna within frees one from self-defeating habits. Such tangible experience quickly clears away misgivings and opens a floodgate of inspiration and happiness in one's life.

Sūta concludes by declaring that for millennia, serious and thoughtful seekers have observed that the bliss of bhakti yoga, firmly grounded in systematic, non-fanatical practices, far surpasses materialism and mental guesswork as a means to fulfillment.

TWO

NĀRADA

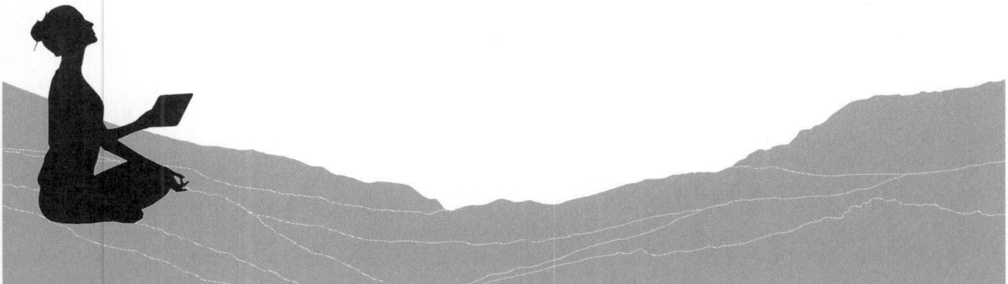

ŚAUNAKA QUESTIONS SŪTA (1-7)

Then Śaunaka, the congregation's leading elder sage,
declared to Sūta, "We who have assembled to engage
in lengthy sacrifice accept your offer to recite
the *Bhāgavat*, as Śukadev once did within your sight.

Could you explain in more detail how Vyās became inspired
to write the *Bhāgavat*, and how the whole event transpired?
We know that Śukadev left home when he was young and fair.
Although he left his clothes behind, he didn't seem to care.

As Vyās ran after Śukadev, stark naked on the path,
some lovely girls dipped in a nearby lake to take their bath.
They didn't blink when Śukadev, the youth, meandered by,
but when they saw Vyās, they covered up and felt quite shy.
Now, Vyās had seen this happen, and he paused there to observe,
'You just ignored my naked son, yet I make you reserved!'
'Your son saw us as spirit, not as flesh," the girls explained,
'and though you're very learned, that's a stage you've not attained.'

When Śukadev had wandered through the vast provincial lands,
he reached the nation's capital. Did people understand?
Did they decide that he was mad, retarded, or just dumb?
How was it that he met the King and *Bhāgavat* was sung?

We know that Śukadev would stay in any given home
just long enough to milk a cow, and then, again, he'd roam.
He only stopped at all, it seems, where other people dwell,
to sanctify the household and the householders as well.

We also know that dying king whom Śukadev addressed,
was strong enough to keep the awful Kali-age repressed.
Now, why would such a king sit down on Gaṇgā's riverside,
give up his throne and take a vow to fast until he died?

Except for certain portions of the ancient Vedic texts,
your knowledge, we believe, is absolute in all respects.
Since you can solve our questions and make everything quite clear,
address us now, dear Sūta. We are very keen to hear."

VYĀS'S DEPRESSION (8-17)

As Sūta smiled respectfully, he said to all the sages,
The great Vyās was born at the conjunction of two ages.[1]
He relished an ascetic's life on Sarasvatī's banks,
until a vision crushed him and his happy spirits sank.

Vyās could see, in meditation, mighty waves of time
imposing great anomalies on all of humankind.
He saw the people troubled and their life spans growing small,
and so he thought as follows, for the wellbeing of all:

"The people of the coming age shall surely be employed
in four career divisions, which nobody can avoid.[2]
However, their discernment of the Veda shall be poor,
so I shall split the Veda into sections one through four.[3]

---

[1] At the end of the Dvapara-yuga (age) and the start of the Kali-yuga (roughly 3000 BC), Vyās resided on the banks of the river Sarasvati.

[2] Four career divisions refer to the *varnāśrama* social system as explained in Chapter 5 of this book.

[3] Veda, which means "knowledge" was Vyās's foundational wisdom text. Subsequently he sought to make it more accessible by dividing it into the *Ṛg*, *Sama*, *Yajur* and *Atharva* Vedas. Later, he added the *Mahabhārata* and other historical texts which are called the fifth Veda.

Since people in the coming age will lose their memory,
I must preserve in writing everything that they will need.
To complement the Vedas, in historical context,
I'll write the *Mahābhārat* and compile Purānic texts."

Vyās fulfilled his promises. The Veda stayed alive
in four distinct divisions, with the histories making five.
Each section was assigned to one esteemed and learned soul,
who mastered his division as preserved on ink and scroll.

Compassionate and wise Vyās, to help the common man,
thus edited the Vedic texts for all to understand.
The wondrous *Mahābhārata*, a historical narration,
uplifted all its readers to the highest destination.

Although he toiled so tirelessly to aid the rank and file,
Vyās would often wonder if his writing was worthwhile.
He knew by codes of dharma that his actions were correct,
but still his heart was troubled, so he started to reflect:

"Now, I have strictly worshipped, with no malice or pretension,
my guru and the Vedas at the altar of tradition.
I wrote the *Mahābhārata*, which surely proved its worth
by uplifting its readers, even those of lower birth.

So from the Vedic point of view, my knowledge is complete,
and still I find my literary triumph bittersweet.
I wonder if, despite my work, I thoughtlessly ignored
the ecstasy of service in devotion to the Lord?"

Vyās sat in depression in the early morning sun
and felt both discontented and confused with what he'd done.

He meditated sadly on that sacred riverside,
when suddenly his saintly guru Nārada arrived.

NĀRADA'S INSTRUCTIONS ON THE *BHĀGAVAT* (18-30)

Saint Nārada, the sage among the gods, sat down and smiled.
He said, "My learned friend, Vyās, has all that you've compiled
about the mind and body as the goals of realization
left you upset and unfulfilled? Is that your situation?"

Vyās replied, "Exactly so! Please tell me why, my lord,
with all my years of sacrifice, why should I feel discord?
Since you're well known for turning up and solving mysteries,
will you inspect my heart and spell out my deficiencies?"

Replied the saintly Nārada, in prompt evaluation,
"Your words on duty, money, sense enjoyment and salvation,[4]
though pleasing to the followers of worldly categories,
have failed to mention Krishna, or elucidate His glories.

Those words describing Krishna clean the heart, as you well know,
while other words are simply sites of pilgrimage for crows.
Wherever crows assemble to debate at length and leisure,
the swan-like sages never take a single moment's pleasure.

And on the other hand, Vyās, those words that just describe
Lord Krishna's names and forms and pastimes revolutionize
the sinful lives of victims of the Kali-age assault.
Enlightened people love such words, though spoken with some fault.

---

[4] In Sanskrit, dharma, *artha*, *kāma* and *mokṣa*, the four cyclical activities of mundane existence.

Philosophy devoid of Krishna has no valid use,
and what to speak of troublesome material pursuits!
Since you are wise and firm in vow and blessed with much esteem,
just write about Lord Krishna, and your work will be redeemed.

For as the wind can rock a boat with anchor unsecured,
to fail to mention Krishna leaves a reader's mind disturbed.
Your readers cite religion as they sin their lives away,
and you have inadvertently encouraged them this way.

Who else but learned experts who renounce all worldly vice
can ever understand the deeper truth of human life?
You surely have such gifts, Vyās, and I find you most fit
to narrate Krishna's pastimes for your readers' benefit.

A soul pursuing Krishna may attempt to serve but fail,
yet such a person still exceeds the worldly who prevail,
for Krishna will protect the deathless soul of one who tries,
while one who chases money loses everything and dies.

So learned, thoughtful people, philosophically inclined,
do not pursue material success of any kind.
Enjoyment of the senses can be found both near and far
and comes to us as troubles do, unwanted as they are.

A soul who hears and learns of Krishna never undergoes
another birth in ignorance, and this is why it's so:
If only once one relishes the touch of Krishna's feet,
he never can forget it or find anything more sweet.

Lord Krishna is in everything, yet He remains aloof,
and relishes His pastimes, which are pure and absolute.
Good soul, you're meant to help the world. Your time has come. Now please,
write more about Śri Krishna and His sweet activities.

For learned circles long ago concluded without doubt
that souls imprisoned in this world and wanting to get out
through sacrifice, austerity, or prayers that start with "oṁ"
should rather hear of Krishna, who is praised in chosen poems.

NĀRADA'S HISTORY (31-50)

To give you an example, I'll describe my former life.
My poor and honest mother was, in fact, nobody's wife.
One summer she and I were hosts to several learned priests
who lived with us and studied till the monsoon showers ceased.

The priests were kind and merciful, and I was well-behaved.
Quite often I would listen as those great Vedāntists gave
enlightened explanations of Lord Krishna's famous deeds.
I gained a taste to hear and felt my ignorance recede.

To hear from those beloved sages purified my soul.
I mimicked them and kept my senses calm and well-controlled.
The day the sages left, they smiled at me with eyes agleam,
and taught me confidentially that Krishna is Supreme."

Vyās inquired, "How did you spend your life after that day?
Your body now is deathless. Did that body pass away?
Since time will always vanquish things a person does or knows,
how is it you recall details so well from long ago?

Said Nārada, "The sages went away, and I remained
entangled with my mother by affection's heavy chains.
She struggled on and managed to send me to school somehow,
until a serpent killed her when she went to milk a cow.

Lord Krishna can show mercy in a way we don't expect.
Left homeless and an orphan, I turned north and simply trekked
through cities, towns and villages with gardens, farms, and glens.
At last, I reached a mountain forest shunned by other men.

I felt quite tired and found a lake where I could drink and bathe.
Refreshed, I saw a banyan tree and sat beneath its shade.
Remembering the sages, in that desolate location,
I kindled my intelligence and practiced meditation.

I fixed the thought of Krishna's lotus feet within my mind
till love for Him infused me and my eyes were teary blind.
And then within my heart I saw the Lord, as I see you,
but in that blissful moment I abruptly lost my view.

Arising as one does when something valuable is missed,
again I tried to see the Lord with childish eagerness.
But failing to recover Him, I sat and cried in grief.
Observing me, the unseen Lord said this, to my relief:

"Dear Nārada, within this life, you've seen the last of Me.
The vision you've been granted is reserved for persons free
of any worldly hankering. And still, you shall be graced,
for you'll forget mundane desire. You've had a higher taste.

My child, when you serve Me, I shall reciprocate in kind,
by bringing you to My abode when you leave yours behind.
Become a pure, devoted soul. Be firm and never sway.
The universe may come and go, but pure devotion stays."

The gracious Lord withdrew His voice and, gratefully, I bowed.
I left that place in bliss, repeating Krishna's names aloud.
Discarding all formalities and brimming with goodwill,
I humbly traveled through the world, serene and quite fulfilled.

I stayed absorbed in Krishna-thought. My heart grew pure and free.
And then, as lightening and its flash take place concurrently,
I lost that mortal body, an affliction I don't miss,
and entered my eternal form, enlightened and in bliss.

And since the dawn of this creation, by Lord Krishna's grace,
I freely travel everywhere, through heaven, earth and space.
While chanting Krishna's holy names, my tuneful vina[5] hums,
and through this sound, within my heart, Lord Krishna always comes.

Attachments left me helpless in a troubled worldly ocean
until I found the solid boat of chanting and devotion.
While grueling yoga practice keeps attachment somewhat checked,
To hear of Krishna's pastimes thrills the soul in all respects.

O sinless Vyās, I now have answered all that you have asked,
so take it for your benefit and ponder your next task.
Please write about Lord Krishna's deeds, which you can well express
and give your readers freedom from material distress."

[5] A simple stringed instrument used to accompany chanting.

While vibrating his vina, Nārada then took his leave.
Vyās began to meditate, and soon the sage perceived
how people serve their bodies and ignore their spirit souls
and try to lord it over what the Lord alone controls.

While souls encased in matter suffer superficial pain,
the sound of Krishna's pastimes quickly makes it go away.
Since people do not know this fact, the learned Vyās compiled
the pastimes of Lord Krishna in his clear and simple style.
If one will simply hear this book, the cause of all one's fears—
the sense that soul and flesh are one—completely disappears.

Just after he compiled this book, the *Bhāgavat* by name,
Vyās taught it to Śukadev, his son, who had attained
to perfect knowledge of the soul, with nothing overlooked.
So why, you ask, would Śukadev explore this vast new book?

The learned Śukadev thought God was formless as the breeze
until he heard of Krishna from the kindly devotees.
Yes, even liberated persons, free of all desire,
still hanker after Krishna, whom they naturally admire.

STRATEGY #2: ASK A GURU

Before writing the *Bhāgavat Purāṇa*, Vyās had already written many other books. Despite his literary accomplishments, he was feeling morose. One day, while he was pondering the cause of his dissatisfaction, his teacher Nārada came by and aptly diagnosed the problem: in carefully presenting the various corollary principles of religion, Vyas had neglected the essence—a description of the Supreme Himself. Satisfaction comes from bhakti-yoga, Nārada explained, connecting to the Supreme through devotional service. Nārada therefore advised Vyās to increase his bhakti-yoga practice by writing more directly about Krishna.

Nārada then narrated his own story of how hearing about Krishna from advanced devotees changed his life in an epic and positive way. Vyās took these words of his guru to heart and wrote the *Bhāgavat Purāna*, and his despondency turned to blissful satisfaction.

Like Vyās, we, too, may experience bouts of depression. In cases of severe depression, the first modern-day solution is to seek professional help from psychologists who can talk us through our problems. In the ancient Vedic culture, this role would be filled by one's guru.

What exactly does a guru, or spiritual teacher, do? Before we can discuss this question, we must consider what a guru is. Just as a mental health professional needs to be qualified by earning credentials from a recognized institution, a real guru must have three qualifications, summarized in the acronym LAW:

- **Lineage.** Learning from a guru is a prerequisite for spiritual enlightenment, so a guru must have also had a guru from a lineage of gurus coming before.
- **Action.** Gurus must 'walk the talk' and actually embody the practices and truths they teach.

- **Words.** As with any accomplished person, gurus must know, understand and speak in accordance with recognized textbooks in their field.

Sadly, unlike modern psychiatry, in spiritual matters there are no laws or regulators to verify one's credentials. As a result, the 'guru business' is full of fakes. An intelligent student of yoga should carefully understand the above points before choosing a mentor. By making an educated choice, we can avoid selecting on impulse or sentiment someone who later disappoints us.

How do we find a genuine guru? Tradition says that the appearance of a guru in our lives happens automatically when we are ready, so we don't need to conduct a huge search. Nor do we need to rush. We can begin our bhakti practice by chanting appropriate mantras and reading authorized bhakti texts. For instance, the books of Srila A.C. Bhaktivedanta Swami Prabhupada, including scholarly, in-depth translations of the *Bhagavad-gītā* and *Bhāgavat Purāṇa*, have proven especially helpful for seriously aspiring bhakti-yogīs. By learning more from these books about the qualifications of a genuine spiritual guide, we prepare ourselves for the eventual appearance of our own personal guru. Prior to that pivotal event, we may also have many instructing gurus who help us along the way.

The word guru literally means 'heavy,' as in one who is heavy with knowledge. A qualified guru understands the science of bhakti and how to apply it. Since most forms of misery stem from ignorance and entanglement in the material way of life, a genuine guru can uplift us from depression by enlightening us with transcendental knowledge and by teaching us how to spiritualize our vocation, family responsibilities and hobbies.

Fortunately for Vyās, Nārada is a genuinely qualified guru. By the end of their discussion, Vyās is once again energized, clear and happily pursuing his beloved writing.

THREE

DRAUPADĪ

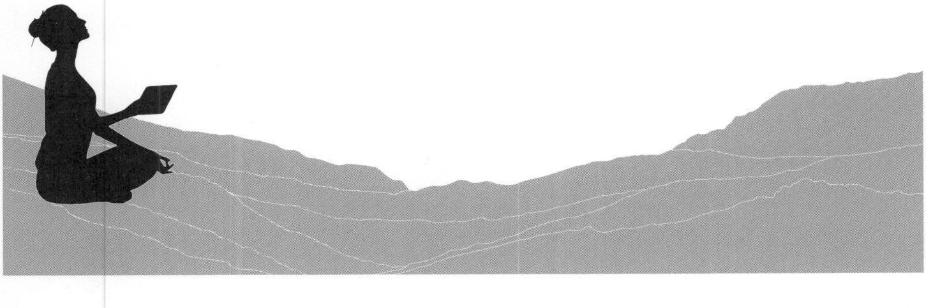

SETTING THE SCENE (1-6)

You now have learned about this book and something of its theme,
so I'll describe Lord Krishna. Let us first set out the scene.
We'll hear of Pāṇḍu's[1] sons and of the kingdom they acquired
and learn about the heir who took their throne when they retired.

The *Mahābhārata* describes the Kurukṣetra war.
In victory, the sons of Pāṇḍu managed to restore
their father's kingdom, stolen by Duryodhana and clan,
who coerced righteous Droṇa to assist their evil plan.

Duryodhana was nearly dead. In mortal pain he lay,
and Droṇa and his other warriors all had passed away.
But Aśvattāmā, son of Droṇa, loyal to the end,
conceived a wicked plot to bring Duryodhana revenge.

Then Pāṇḍu's sons, victorious, as evening brought some peace,
sent off their five young warrior sons to spend the night at ease.
Within the darkness of their quarters Aśvattāmā crept
and grimly cut their heads off even as their fathers slept.

Then Aśvattāmā rushed to his beloved master's side
so he could see the youthful skulls and touch them as he died.
Duryodhana just cried aloud to feel the children's hair,
for they were all his nephews and the family's only heirs.

Poor Draupadī, the mother of the boys, could not contain
her anguish upon learning that all five were cruelly slain.
Her mighty husband Arjuna embraced his wife and said,
"You soon shall bathe while standing on this Aśvattāmā's head!"

[1] See the glossary for details about the many persons from the *Mahābhārata* briefly mentioned here.

THE CLASH OF ULTIMATE WEAPONS (7-12)

Arjuna settled Draupadī, picked up his fearsome bow,
and rode off with Lord Krishna to fulfill his solemn oath.
Observing from a distance, Aśvattāmā turned and fled,
but seeing he was trapped, the rogue abruptly stopped and said,

"What else but the brahmāstra can protect my body now?
Should I release it with my mantras? I do not know how
its nuclear explosion can be harnessed or withdrawn.
It seems I have no other choice. I must invoke this bomb."

On seeing the brahmāstra's brilliance hurtling his way,
the mystified Arjuna stopped his chariot and prayed:
"Invincible Lord Krishna, O most powerful and wise,
just what is this effulgence that is blistering my eyes?"

"Watch out—it's a brahmāstra!" called out Krishna in reply.
"That scoundrel Aśvattāmā threw it, fearing he would die.
You must send your brahmāstra to offset what he has done.
Now quickly throw your own, Arjuna. Answer Droṇa's son!"

Arjuna murmured mantras and touched water with his palm.
While circling Lord Krishna, he cast off his deadly bomb.
As his brahmāstra countered Aśvattāmā's in mid-air,
the two brahmāstras scorched the earth and heavens with their glare.

Arjuna saw the galaxy about to catch afire,
and withdrew both brahmāstras, as Lord Krishna had desired.
His angry eyes like copper suns arising in the east,
Arjuna tied up Aśvattāmā like a squirming beast.

AŚVATTĀMĀ PUNISHED (13-22)

As Krishna turned a thoughtful glance to Arjuna He said,
"What will you do with someone who cut off your children's heads?
A righteous warrior never kills a person drunk or mad,
or women, fools, or servants—what to speak of sleeping lads.

This wretched Aśvattāmā sinned in such a dreadful way,
he'll only suffer later if you let him walk away.
The fool displeased his master. He's the ashes of his clan,
and Draupadī expects his head. Arjuna, kill this man."

Arjuna could not bring himself to take the sinner's life.
Instead, he brought the bound-up Aśvattāmā to his wife.
Confronting her sons' murderer through teary, reddened eyes,
the gentle Draupadī said this, to everyone's surprise:

"Please cut his ropes, Arjuna. He's your guru's only son.
His father was your teacher. Just consider all he's done.
Now Droṇa lives on in his son, his widows' only joy.
Please spare her all the tears I shed before my lifeless boys.

My wise and mighty husband, Droṇa's son must be released.
for now that we are rulers, can we kill the sons of priests?
If you kill him, the other priests will curse our realm to fall.
When kings are gone, the thieves grow strong, and chaos rules all."

Arjuna looked at Yudhiṣṭhir, his elder, king and lord,
who thoughtfully heard Draupadī and nodded in accord.
He felt that everything she said was scriptural and fair,
infused with mercy, glorious, and spoken without airs.

Throughout the vicious war, the sons of Pāṇḍu all survived.
Now Sahadev and Nakula, the youngest of the five,
assented with Arjuna, Draupadī, and Yudhiṣṭhir.
But Bhīma shouted, "Kill the wretch! His sin was too severe!"

While glancing at Arjuna, Krishna smiled a bit and said,
"Now Bhīma must be satisfied. He wants this sinner dead.
Arjuna, you must also please your ruler and your wife,
who want to see this fallen priest preserve his sinful life."

On hearing these conflicting words, Arjuna took the hint
and sliced off Aśvattāmā's hair and sacred ornaments.
Now Aśvattāmā's strength was gone. He sat as in a daze.
Arjuna cut his ropes and drove the wretched fool away.

Such punishment just suited mighty Droṇa's only son,
for he remained alive, and yet his powers were undone.
The Pāṇḍavas and Draupadī now turned their thoughts instead
to dealing with the rituals required for the dead.

A FINAL ATTACK (23-32)

The ladies led the mourners to the Gaṇgā's banks that day,
where all of the survivors then lamented, prayed and bathed.
Old Dhṛtarāṣṭra, Duryodhana's father, also came.
Lord Krishna gathered everyone and spoke to ease their pain:

"We must remember nature's laws will always take control,
destroying all our well-laid plans and taking heavy tolls.
So, don't lament; these souls live on. Your loved ones have replaced
their old bodies with new ones in a better, happy place.

Duryodhana sinned greatly when he stole his cousins' throne,
and he has died along with those who made his cause their own.
Queen Draupadī's assailants have all paid the final price.[2]
Now let us help King Yudhiṣṭhir with Vedic sacrifice."

The kings and sages present offered Krishna heartfelt prayers.
Lord Krishna thanked them graciously. But then, as He prepared
to climb aboard his chariot, He heard a desperate cry
from Uttarā, the princess, who was running to His side.

Her husband Abhimanyu was Arjuna's greatest son,
a brilliant young commander who was loved by everyone.
But in the Kurukṣetra war, a gang of kings conspired
to butcher him unfairly, and he gallantly expired.

The fair young widow Uttarā was terrified and called,
"Lord Krishna, my Protector, best of mystics, Lord of all.
Protect me, Lord, protect me! No one else can grant this boon.
The child of my dead husband lies imperiled in my womb.
I feel a new brahmāstra's heat descending upon me,
and targeting my embryo to end our dynasty.
It comes from Aśvattāmā, for he's furious and wild.
Please let it kill my body, Lord, but not abort my child."

Lord Krishna quickly turned His gaze on all of Pāṇḍu's sons,
but Uttarā's dilemma left them mystified and stunned.
Nakula, Bhīma, Sahadev, Arjun and Yudhiṣṭhir
all quickly seized their weapons as they looked about in fear.

---

[2] Duryodhana and his brothers once publicly insulted Draupadī by dragging her by the hair before an assembly.

Now in the war preceding this astounding final act,
Lord Krishna had renounced all weapons, even when attacked.
But when this mortal peril to His devotee occurred,
Lord Krishna drew His razor-disc, prepared to break His word.

Lord Krishna saw the sons of Pāṇḍu looking unprepared
to counter the brahmāstra aimed precisely at their heir.
So, He who is the Supersoul and lives in everyone
appeared within the womb alongside Abhimanyu's son.

Although the fierce brahmāstra can't be checked in any way,
Lord Krishna, by His very presence, stopped its deadly rays.
Oh, do not be surprised, dear friends, for in His wondrous form,
Lord Krishna starts and stops us all—yet He is never born.

STRATEGY #3: ACT COMPASSIONATELY

Draupadī grieved so much upon losing all five of her sons that when her husband Arjuna promised to bring her the decapitated head of their murderer, Aśvattāmā, she did not object. Yet when he actually captured Aśvattāmā, the son of his beloved teacher, Arjuna could not bring himself to execute him. Instead, he tied him up and brought him to Draupadī so she could decide his fate. To everyone's surprise, Draupadī spared his life, reasoning that she did not want Aśvattāmā's respected mother to suffer the pain she felt upon losing her sons.

Draupadī's compassion for Aśvattāmā's mother overpowered her anger toward him. Would we have been so sensitive to another's feelings?

Practicing bhakti-yoga awakens compassion, both for ourselves and for others. As spirits struggling in the material world, we have built up walls of ego to protect ourselves from being hurt. As we connect with Krishna, we gain a trust in His protection that allows us to slowly lower those walls, recognizing that we only built them in the first place out of unfounded fears.

We then see ourselves as we are, like scared children, and we see why we have adopted this needless defensive attitude. This experience frees us from the crushing burden of maintaining pretenses and allows us to see others as fellow travelers caught in the same situation, invoking sincere, warm feelings of empathy. As Srila Prabhupada succinctly put it, "Compassion for the eternal soul is self-realization."[3]

In further describing self-realization, the *Bhagavad-gītā* explains that for the soul there is no birth and death, nor having once been does the soul ever cease to be. However, mistakenly identified with a temporary mate-

[3] *Bhagavad-gītā As It Is* by Śrila A.C. Bhaktivedanta Swami Prabhupada, 2.1

rial body, the soul becomes attached to material things and dies in that compromised frame of mind. Bhakti-yoga breaks the cycle of birth and death by helping us replace material desires with spiritual desires. When we have no material desires, we have no need for a material body. Instead, our desire to serve Krishna frees us to enter the spiritual world, the Supreme abode of Krishna, which is described in some detail later in the *Bhāgavat Purāṇa*. The joy of freedom from birth and death can be directly perceived in this life. To experience this joy fulfills us like nothing else, and giving it to others is the greatest act of compassion.

Our spiritual progress can be measured by how much our compassion for others has awakened. When our care for others overcomes our knee-jerk instinct to protect our ego, we have come to a high level of spiritual consciousness attained only by true saints such as Draupadī. In the meantime, we can at least understand theoretically where the pursuit of spiritual life will take us. Even if her attitude seems far beyond us now, we can learn from Draupadī's example that compassion is attainable. Seeing a highway road sign does not mean we have reached our destination, yet it comforts us to know we are on the right track.

Without understanding oneself as a soul and an eternal servant of the Supreme, compassion can at best be physical. Helping the poor to eat or the disadvantaged to learn shows one's decency as a human being. Although such acts of kindness may help people live more comfortably in this life, one who is ignorant of the soul can do nothing to address deeper problems. This story illustrates the point:

Once, a man at the beach rushed into the pounding surf to save a woman's drowning husband. After some time, he returned and graciously presented the hysterical woman with her husband's wet shirt. "Where is my husband?" she cried. Replied the hero, "I could not save him, but I did save his shirt."

So it is with those whose compassion extends only to the physical body. The material body is not the person, just a temporary covering of the soul. The soul is the real person, struggling and suffering in the cycle of birth and death. Keeping others physically comfortable until they die, although kind, does not solve the person's deeper problem of having to come back to do it all over again.

Practicing compassion is a great joy. As Shakespeare wrote in *The Merchant of Venice*:

> The quality of mercy is not strained; It droppeth as the gentle rain from heaven upon the place beneath. It is twice blest; it blesseth him that gives and him that takes: 'T is mightiest in the mightiest; it becomes the throned monarch better than his crown.

Though we may not wear crowns and wield royal power, all of us souls in human bodies do hold life-and-death power over animals. Understanding animals as living beings like us, sentenced by their past deeds to an inferior birth, we can see them with compassion, as fellow sons and daughters of the Supreme. The mindless habit of murdering animals needlessly for food, when ample nutrition is easily available from non-violent sources, destroys our compassion and deprives us of higher spiritual knowledge. It also reflects a heartless attitude toward Mother Earth, for according to the United Nations, the meat industry does more damage to the environment than all of mankind's transportation combined.[4]

Bhakti-yogīs often observe how compassionately some people treat one animal (their pet) and how thoughtlessly they treat another (their lunch). The science of bhakti brings one to a consistent appreciation of life characterized by a deep compassion for all souls, no matter what kind of

---

[4] *Livestock's Long Shadow – Environmental Issues and Options.* Food and Agriculture Organisation. ISBN 92-5-105571-8.

temporary body they inhabit.

Acting on this spiritual vision benefits others and benefits ourselves by improving our health, our planet and our peace of mind. As the ancient *Śrī Iśopaniṣad* says, "One who always sees all living entities as spiritual sparks, in quality one with the Supreme, becomes a true knower of things. What, then, can be illusion or anxiety for such a person?"[5]

Compassion is, indeed, 'twice blessed.'

---

[5] *Śrī Iśopaniṣad* by Srila A.C. Bhaktivedanta Swami Prabhupada, text 7.

FOUR

KUNTĪ

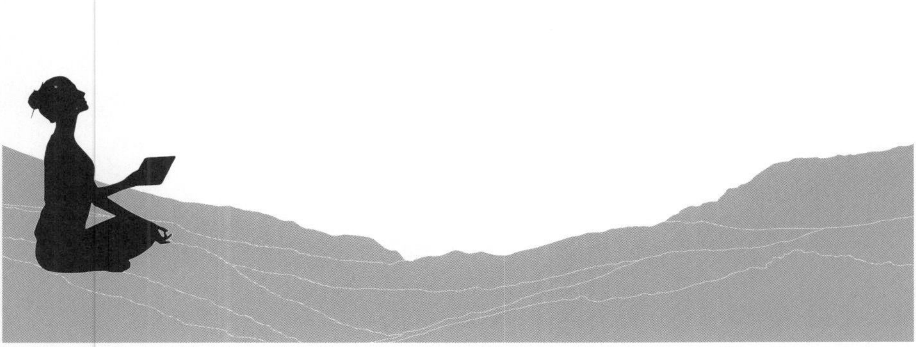

THE PRAYERS OF QUEEN KUNTĪ (1-20)

As Kuntī, Pāṇḍu's widow, watched Lord Krishna's wondrous act,
she worried He would leave them without ever coming back.
Indeed, His splendid chariot stood ready to depart.
Approaching her beloved Krishna, Kuntī spoke her heart:

"Oh best among all persons, Krishna, my respects to You.
Almighty time and nature never govern what You do.
Lord Krishna, You reside within, without and in between
each atom in creation, and yet You are never seen.

As one cannot distinguish expert actors in a play,
mistaking them for characters they skillfully portray,
a fool observes You, Krishna, but can never truly see,
for You have cast a curtain over Your divinity.

My Lord, You come to propagate the yoga of devotion
to all the learned sages who have understood the notion
that soul is not the body, which the common folk don't see.
So how then can we simple women know You perfectly?

I therefore simply bow to you, the most beloved son
of Vasudev and Devakī, so dear to everyone.
As Nanda's lovely cowherd son, Govinda, You arouse
enjoyment in our senses and contentment in the cows.

The lotus-like depression on Your abdomen adorns
the lovely lotus garland, Krishna, draped about Your form.
Your cooling lotus glances make the imagery complete,
including all the lotus marks embellishing Your feet.

You rescued Mother Devakī, O master of the senses,
when evil Kaṁsa jailed her and made numerous offenses.
You similarly rescued all my sons, O Lord, and me
throughout a constant series of extreme calamities.

Duryodhana first poisoned us, then burned our house as well.
He banished us where cannibals and deadly tigers dwell.
When he abused Queen Draupadī, my Lord, we weren't alone,
and now You've stopped the dangerous weapon Aśvattāmā's thrown.

So many times You rescued us from imminent disaster.
I therefore ask of You, my Lord, O Universal Master,
may all of these disasters come again, for when they do,
You also come before us, and our birth and death are through.

You don't come for materialists who endlessly aspire
to build a family name or to fulfill some deep desire
for opulence, attractiveness or high-level degrees.
But one without such passions, Lord, attracts You easily.

For You belong to those who are materially low
and You remain above these worldly things that come and go.
Lord Krishna, no one interrupts Your deep tranquility,
including those who seek to merge with Your identity.

Lord Krishna, You are time itself, with neither start nor end.
Lord Krishna, You are everything. You're everybody's friend,
for as the lord of everyone, Your kindness falls like rain.
You bless all people equally, yet foolish men complain.

Imagining You favor some while others You reject,
such persons think You human, but their views are incorrect.

Of course, Your deeds bewilder us; You work but never act.
It seems that You are born, but you are life itself, in fact.

How could the cowherd queen Yasoda bind You with a knot
when, living as her foster son, You broke her butter pot?
Your childish black mascara ran, awash in frightened tears,
despite the fact that fear itself departs when You appear.

Some say that You have come to bless the Yadu dynasty,
just as the hills of Malaya are blessed by sandal trees.
And others say that Vasudev's and Devakī's desire
persuaded You to be their son and save them as required.

And others say Brahmā observed the sinking boat-like earth,
and prayed for Your protection, which in turn invoked Your birth.
Still others claim You come for those in hedonist decay,
so they may serve and worship You and change their sinful ways.

For anyone who hears and chants Your pastimes and Your name,
or simply feels great happiness when others do the same,
will surely gain the audience of Your soft lotus feet,
and stop the rounds of birth and death that otherwise repeat.

Will You ascend this chariot and leave us here today,
when we depend on You to drive our enemies away?
If You leave, both our kingdom and the Yadu's will subside.
Like bodies that have lost their souls, we all shall quickly die.

Our rivers, hills and seas deliver gems and opulence.
Fine grains and herbs enrich our towns, all due to Your kind glance.
The soft impressions of Your footsteps beautify our realm,
but if You leave, our kingdom will become an empty shell.

I beg You, Krishna, universal source of energy,
to cut these ropes of love that bind me to my family.
As Gaṇgā's waters ever flow directly to the sea,
allow my love to always flow to You exclusively."

KING YUDHIṢṬHIRA'S DESPAIR (21-25)

Lord Krishna smiled enchantingly at Kuntī's heartfelt pleas,
and took some time to comfort her and put her mind at ease.
Again His chariot arrived, but as He turned to board,
King Yudhiṣṭhir cried, "Krishna!" as he tearfully implored,

"Lord Krishna, You have counseled me that I have done no wrong,
And so have Vyās and other sages, citing Vedic psalms.
And yet, I feel the ghastly sin of war upon my head.
I'm meant for serving others, but I've slaughtered them instead.

The boys, the friends, the priests, and all the elders of our clan
have died to fill the wishes of a single selfish man.
Though I may take a million births again and yet again,
I will forever suffer the reactions of my sin.

The scriptures say a king may kill to save society,
but this injunction doesn't lessen my atrocity.
I've left a host of widows, an outrageous, evil act,
that no goodwill or sacrifice will ever counteract.

The sacrifice of animals, though they may be revived,
will never compensate for all these wasted human lives.
How can a filter made of mud make muddy water clean?
How can a pot defiled by wine by wine become redeemed?"

STRATEGY #4: SET SPIRITUAL PRIORITIES

Queen Kuntī first lost her husband. Later, she and her sons were cheated out of their kingdom. Exiled to the forest, they suffered a long series of setbacks and grueling challenges before finally winning back the kingdom that was rightfully theirs. Through all these difficulties, Kuntī depended completely on Krishna, and Krishna, responding to her devotion, always remained nearby like a guardian angel. When everything was set right again and Krishna was confident that Kuntī's family was safe, He prepared to leave. Pained at the thought of separation from Krishna, Kuntī asked Him to bring back all their difficulties if that's what it would take for Him to remain by their side.

Although Kuntī's family members were themselves saints, she was so devoted to Krishna that she asked Him to help her redirect her love for anyone else to Him alone. It's easy to see why Queen Kuntī's beautiful expressions of devotion make her a famous, exemplary bhakti-yogī. Beginners in bhakti are advised to learn from her deep heartfelt spiritual love.

Now, what about us? If we were in Kuntī's place, would we want an easy, comfortable life without Krishna or an austere and challenging life with Krishna? Of course, it's not necessarily one or the other. Still, we do need to set our priorities, because at some point in our lives we will all face this choice: do we make material success our goal and use spare time for spiritual growth, or do we make spiritual success our goal and do the minimum required to meet our material responsibilities?

Most of us tend to make the default decision to satisfy ourselves physically first with a sincere promise to deal with spirituality immediately afterwards. Though this strategy seems practical, it comes with obvious risks. For one thing, most people are never satisfied materially. As soon as we fulfill one desire, another pressing desire sprouts up. Another pitfall: when we get what we want materially, we may wonder, "Why bother with spirituality?"

For example, a wealthy man named Harold once came upon unexpected reverses and desperately prayed to God, "If You will just revive my business, I promise to sell my mansion and give all the proceeds to the church."

After some months of struggle, Harold's business again prospered. He was overjoyed until, abruptly, he remembered his promise.

The next day a strange ad appeared in the real estate pages:

Mansion for sale: Ten landscaped acres, six bedrooms, four baths, pool, six-car garage. $1.00.

To those who called to ask if it was a misprint Harold replied, "No, it's just a dollar. But there is one condition: you have to buy my cat as well."

"How much is your cat?"

"$2,999,999.00."

After eventually selling both the mansion and the cat, Harold slipped into church and put a dollar in the collection plate.

If we follow Harold's example and make our spiritual practice contingent on material success, our spiritual life is in jeopardy, for material success is not everyone's destiny. Yet from our earliest days most of us are pushed toward material success. Thus especially in today's materialistic society, the only way to maintain a healthy spiritual life is to make it our top priority.

Some thoughtful people would like to pursue spiritual life but lack the know-how. The clear and scientific bhakti process can help. Not only does bhakti offer simple, powerful practices such as hearing and chanting, but it takes inner development one step further: it teaches us how to turn our material activities into spiritual activities by making the Supreme's pleasure a priority over our own. Does pleasing the Supreme first leave us with the short end of the stick? Not at all! Through bhakti yoga, pleasing the Supreme, we experience an enduring happiness far more satisfying than anything material .

This sublime spiritual truth applies to all of our activities. The *Bhagavad-gītā* gives the example of eating: we can put together our favorite meal and wolf it down, or we can prepare our favorite vegetarian meal and offer it to Krishna for His pleasure. The philosophy is logical: only God can create food—man can't make even a grain of rice—so instead of thoughtlessly taking food and perhaps remembering to say, "Thanks," bhaktas first offer their food back to Him. He's a Person and, if food is offered with love, He accepts it. Practicing this simple daily act opens an unexpected world of bliss.

Seeking first to please the Supreme in all aspects of life creates an astonishing sense of joy and well-being. One young lady recently said, "I hate washing dishes at home. But when I wash Krishna's dishes at the Bhakti Center, it's so much fun." This newcomer quickly learned how to spiritualize her cooking (and dishwashing) at home as well.

As we read about the joy of bhakti, some doubts may pop up in our minds. If I shift my priority to spiritual growth, aren't I putting myself at risk materially? How will I feel in the course of spiritual growth if I suffer some calamity, such as poverty, disease or loss of loved ones? Unlike the highly advanced Queen Kuntī, will such setbacks make me blame, question or become bitter to the very notion of a Supreme controller?

In the sixth chapter of *Bhagavad-gītā*, after hearing how to perform classic yoga and meditation, the student Arjuna asks his teacher Krishna a similar question. What will happen if I give up my material life and follow the spiritual path but then fail? If that happens I'm just a useless failure materially and spiritually. In reply, Krishna assures us that any effort toward spirituality is never lost, for unlike material accomplishments, spiritual growth stays with the soul after death, assuring at the very least a more conducive birth in the next lifetime.

Nevertheless, there will be downsides to prioritizing spiritual life. Perhaps the most predictable is pushback from materially prioritized people. As Jesus famously said upon returning to Nazareth, "A prophet is not without honor except in his hometown, among his relatives and in his own house." Going even deeper in the same vein, the great bhakta Mādhavendra Puri said, "Let the sharp moralist accuse me of being illusioned; I do not mind. Experts in religious activities may slander me as being misled, friends and relatives may call me frustrated, my brothers may call me a fool, the wealthy may point me out as mad and learned philosophers may assert that I am much too proud. Still my mind does not budge an inch from the determination to serve Krishna, though I am unable to do it."

Yes, putting spirituality first is not without material risk. On the other hand, putting externals first in an uncertain world is even riskier, for it means we are gambling with both our inner and outer happiness. For this reason, as we read earlier (Chapter 2, text 27), Nārada advised his disciple Vyās and all intelligent people to look inward first:

> The learned, thoughtful people, philosophically inclined,
> do not pursue material success of any kind.
> Enjoyment of the senses can be found both near and far
> and comes to us as troubles do, unwanted as they are.

Because happiness and distress are both inevitable in this world, bhakti-yogīs put their energy into first pleasing the Supreme, through any or all of the nine bhakti practices. Giving our inner life first priority lifts us above the ups and downs of the external world.

A guru can show the aspiring bhakta how to adjust nearly any profession, vocation and family situation so that pleasing the Supreme becomes one's first priority, just as Kuntī so beautifully expresses. Though contrary to instinct and habit, the great joy and satisfaction that comes from first pleasing the Supreme is a subjective fact that anyone can experience—if one is objective enough to at least try it.

FIVE

BHĪṢMA

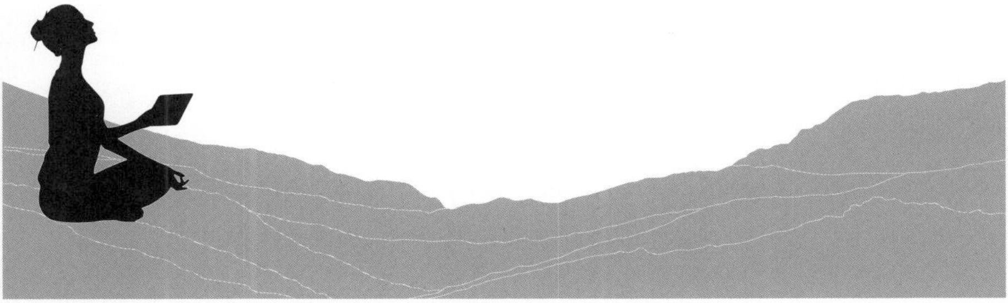

BHĪṢMA'S BED OF ARROWS (1-13)

As Yudhiṣṭhir lamented in this pitiable way,
upon the nearby battlefield the dying Bhīṣma lay.
In deep depression, Yudhiṣṭhir proceeded to his side
to ask for more instruction as his learned elder died.

Great Bhīṣma was the grandfather, the eldest Kuru man,
who trained both groups of warriors in the fratricidal clan.
He tried to sway Duryodhana to walk the path of peace
then fought for him reluctantly, yet fiercely as a beast.

Although he knew Duryodhana could never hope to win,
because he had been obligated, Bhīṣma served his whims.
However, in the battle, Bhīṣma's goal became quite clear:
to die at Krishna's hand, though He was just a charioteer.

Arjuna wouldn't battle Bhīṣma, whom he so adored,
but no one else could answer Bhīṣma's fury in the war.
Lord Krishna urged Arjuna on until he pulled his bow
and fired deadly arrows, laying mighty Bhīṣma low.

Now Bhīṣma had been blessed in life that he could chose the time
when he would leave his body and this mortal world behind.
So Bhīṣma lay, his body pierced with many arrow shafts
while waiting for the sun to take the proper northern path.

When Yudhiṣṭhir and many sages thereafter arrived
it seemed that Bhīṣma was a god just fallen from the sky.
Lord Krishna and Arjuna came, with many kings and priests,
and Bhīṣma thanked them all and said, to mitigate their grief:

"Dear Yudhiṣṭhir, what suffering and wrongs you have endured!
Though you and all your brothers should have died, you all observed
the principles of righteousness, and thus you gained the help
of saintly souls, religion, and almighty God Himself.

Your mother also suffered as a widow with five sons.
She suffered even more through all the battles you have won.
Inevitable time has so disrupted all your lives,
for time can push a planet as if vapor through the skies.

Yes, time ordains our destinies and cannot be undone.
How else could so much suffering descend on Pāṇḍu's sons?
King Yudhiṣṭhir, the righteous? Mighty Bhīma with his mace?
And what of dear Arjuna, whom Lord Krishna ever graced!

Although the great philosophers forever guess and muse,
the plans of higher powers leave them thoroughly confused.
Now Yudhiṣṭhir, you must take charge, as Krishna wants you to,
and guide the helpless citizens who all depend on you.

The Lord Himself, the greatest person, stands within your midst.
Without Krishna, this world of ours would not even exist.
He covers your perception, so you don't know Him in truth,
but Nārada and others know that He is Absolute.

You thought Krishna your counselor, your cousin and your peer.
He served you as an envoy and Arjuna's charioteer.
Though Krishna sits in every heart, impartial, kind and wise,
He's come to comfort his devoted servant as he dies.

Oh Krishna, You can free the minds of those who chant Your name,
releasing them from karma as they quit their mortal frame.

Oh Krishna, You of lovely face with eyes like rosy dawn,
please smile on me and wait for me today as I pass on."

ORGANIZING SOCIETY (14-30)

His audience deemed Bhīṣma's words appealing and profound.
Despite the many sages present on the battleground,
King Yudhiṣṭhir, at Krishna's touch, asked Bhīṣma to explain
the wisdom he would need to rule and build a thriving reign.
The smiling Bhīṣma nodded, and he seemed to be in bliss.
Reclining on his bed of arrows, Bhīṣma offered this:

"A good king never lets the people live the lives of beasts,
who seek only security in food and sex and sleep.
A person must instead aspire to gain these nine credentials:
First, one must never anger over things inconsequential.
One must tell the truth at once in every situation.
One must give out charity without discrimination.
One must bear the wrongdoings that others bring in life.
One must limit intercourse to husband or to wife.
One must be hygienic, both in body and in mind.
One must give up enmity and practice being kind.
One must learn to live in a straightforward, simple way,
and one must always care for his dependents and his aides.

On learning all these basic skills, a person can progress
to one of the four social orders I shall now address.

I'll start with intellectuals, or *brāhmans* as they're known.
They must control their senses, even when they are alone.

Though academic learning is a very useful tool,
it never compensates for the behavior of a fool.

The powerful administrators, *kṣatriyas* by name,
must always give in charity and not accept the same.
Although they know the scriptures, they should always yield to priests,
while shielding the kingdom from invaders, rouges and thieves.

The merchants, known as *vaiṣyas*, are the economic class.
They care for herds of cows, who manufacture milk from grass.
Yes, milk and butter, grains and fruits are truly human wealth,
though slaughtered cows and factories shall finance Kali's hell.

The *śūdras* are the simple class who serve the other three.
so they should be protected and supplied with every need.
If they are left to hoard their funds for gambling, sex and wine,
they'll lead the whole society in decadent decline.

For *śūdras* are like legs on which the social body stands;
the *vaiṣyas* are the stomach who fulfill all its demands.
The *kṣatriyas*, the arms, make sure the body is maintained;
and *brāhmans* are the head. They are the social body's brain.

Although these four professions help society run well,
they are, in fact, material. The scriptures also tell
of spiritual divisions, overlaid on social roles,
that carry people closer to the highest human goal.

The student life, or *brāhmacārī*, helps one realize
material existence is a rascal's paradise.
The *brāhmacārī* makes a peaceful mind his greatest prize,
so he can be detached and go to Krishna when he dies.

The bulk of us, who've yet to fully grasp this goal of life,
move on to be *gṛhasthas* and conjoin as man and wife.
Gṛhasthas work and prosper as they propagate the race,
while realizing Krishna at a somewhat slower pace.

And when their children grow and wed, a man and wife become
a *vānaprastha* couple, for their worldly duty's done.
Instead of just retiring to a cozy rocking chair,
such couples go to holy places, seeking Krishna there.

In course of time a man may take *sannyās*, the final stage,
and leave his wife in care of children who have come of age.
Sannyāsis, full of wisdom gleaned from living many years,
should roam and teach incessantly and conquer every fear.

Now, since the love of Krishna is the highest goal of man,
some *brāhmacaris* take *sannyās* directly, if they can.
In one way or another, as a student, monk or wife,
each person should pursue Lord Krishna all throughout their life.

The students practice sacrifice, for they are young and fresh;
The householders give charity, for they indulge the flesh.
And those retired and those renounced are meant to grow more free
through penance and detachment and divine austerity.

Selecting by his nature from the four orders of toil,
a man may teach or manage, sell, or simply work the soil.
And still, one grows in spirit like the branches from a trunk,
as student or as householder, retired man or monk.

Yes, everyone will flourish in the system I've explained
The four vocations, known as *varṇas*, easily maintain,

the four supporting *aśrams*, or the spiritual divisions.
And all of this is known as the *varṇāśram* social system."

RULING A KINGDOM (31-40)

King Yudhiṣṭhir thanked Bhīṣma for his clear, insightful words
and said, "My learned Grandfather, as now we all have heard
the theory of the system of *varṇāśram* social life,
please tell us what a king must do to see that it's applied."

Said Bhīṣma, with his eyes half-closed, "A monarch always acts
to benefit the people, not to merely take their tax.
Though any king may rightly claim a fourth of people's gains,
the people give it willingly when saintly monarchs reign.

For saintly kings will always help the people they control
to free themselves from birth and death and liberate their souls.
To see to this, a king need not enforce a certain creed;
he simply needs to care for saints and give them what they need.

A proper king must swiftly punish dacoits, crooks and rogues,
so crime will be unthinkable and fully out of vogue.
But in the coming Kali-age, such kings will not be found,
and citizens will vote for crooks who tax them to the ground."

King Yudhiṣṭhir asked, "How do kings direct society
to end the fear of birth and death and live more sensibly?

Said Bhīṣma, "Kings must study how the citizens behave
and help them curb bad habits by instructing them this way:

‘To conquer over anger you must learn how to forgive;
To conquer over crime, do not make plans, but simply live;
To conquer your desires, simple tolerance is best,
and sleepiness is overcome by spiritual zest;
By regulating wishes, you shall conquer fantasies;
By regulating diet, you shall conquer all disease;
By taking help of yoga, you can conquer appetite;
And you can conquer losses choosing friends who are upright.

One conquers over worldliness through knowledge of the soul;
One conquers over lethargy by careful self-control;
One conquers shifty arguments by sticking to the truth;
One conquers useless chattiness by growing more aloof;
One conquers fear by prowess. In this way, self-cultivation
shall lead to perfect knowledge and eventual salvation.

King Yudhiṣṭhir inquired, “Grandsire, does the gentle sex
possess a special role in this societal context?

“Indeed,” said Bhīṣma. “Women can empower and inspire
the greatest of accomplishments from men whom they admire.
This trait makes women stronger and more powerful, you see,
unless they grow unfaithful and commit adultery.
Since unplanned children, born of lust, destroy society,
a sober woman always must maintain her chastity.”

“And finally,” said Bhīṣma, as he struck a closing chord,
“Each citizen must always be a servant of the Lord.
A person who remembers this and sees that God is pleased
shall very quickly manifest all saintly qualities.”

BHĪṢMA'S PASSING (41-52)

Although it's strange a king would question one about to die,
the questions of King Yudhiṣṭhir left Bhīṣma satisfied.
He turned his mind to Krishna, shutting other topics out,
and noted that the sun had slipped into its northern route.
As Bhīṣma saw the proper time had come for his demise,
he fondly gazed at Krishna, who stood smiling at his side.

And then that mighty soldier who won a thousand wars,
whose exploits had already been enshrined in Vedic lore,
who gave a thousand lectures on a thousand different themes,
choked up and spoke his final words to Krishna, the Supreme.

Said Bhīṣma, "Lord, my faculty to think and feel and do
has simply been invested in this world, which Krishna, You
created for us fallen souls attached to worldly treasure.
And yet, my Lord, you also come to bring your servants pleasure.

Your bluish tint and yellow silks and sandal-pasted brow
attract all living entities to see You even now.
How pleasing is Your beauty! As I lie here, I recall
Your pastimes in the battle. I want nothing else at all.

As You drove with Arjuna through the Kuruṣksetra fray,
Your blackish hair turned ashen from the dust the horses raised.
As perspiration wet Your face, my arrows pierced Your skin.
You seemed to love it, Krishna. Oh, to see that sight again!

As Duryodhana's warriors expired by Your glance,
within the heat of battle, You gave Arjuna the chance

to rectify his ignorance and clarify his mind.
Now let Your lotus feet and me forever be aligned.

Before the dreadful battle, You had promised everyone
that You would lift no weapon once the fighting had begun.
But when I fought Arjuna, and his love restrained his bow,
You leapt and snatched a broken wheel and rushed to set me low.
Though nothing can diminish Your eternal form of bliss,
my arrows drew Your blood, and I was careful not to miss.
I wanted You to kill me then and break Your guarantee.
Arjuna, though, demanded one more chance to battle me.
Although the sunset came just then and stopped the incident,
You looked just like a lion who attacks an elephant.
I pray to die recalling You in such a striking mode
and join the other soldiers who returned to Your abode.

Please draw my mind to You, just like the cowherd girls of Vraj.
You danced with them and left them with a lover's ceaseless grudge.
And then you took first worship in the court of Yudhiṣṭhir.
Dear Krishna, I remember all You've done as death draws near.

As men in different countries see a solitary sun,
dear Krishna, you reside within the hearts of everyone.
'These people differ by their bodies,' I had once construed,
but now I see within their hearts, Lord Krishna, only You."

Then Bhīṣma fully turned his gaze and thoughts to Krishna's face
and stopped his speech and breath at this, his chosen time and place.
Beholding Bhīṣma's passing, which was peaceful and sublime,
his audience grew silent, like the birds at evening time.

As men and gods struck kettledrums in praise of Bhīṣma's grace,
a stream of flower petals from the sky adorned his face.
Although he saw that Bhīṣma reached his goal of pure devotion,
King Yudhiṣṭhir was briefly overtaken by emotion.

The sages sang in praise of Krishna from the Vedic hymns,
then left the battlefield for home, immersed in thoughts of Him.
In bitter triumph, Pāṇḍu's sons approached Hastināpur
to comfort those who lost their loved ones in the dreadful war.

Thereafter, Yudhiṣṭhir, the king of great religious fame,
prepared himself to govern just as Bhīṣma had explained.
The aged Dhṛtarāṣṭra helped his nephew take the throne,
and Krishna also came to help before His journey home.

STRATEGY #5: CULTIVATE THE MODE OF GOODNESS

Teachings such as Bhīṣma's in the *Bhāgavat Purāṇa* builds on the basic spiritual teachings of *Bhagavad-gītā*, including its explanation of the powerful influence of the three modes of nature. These modes include:

- Ignorance (*tamo guṇa*), which entices us to obsess with the past, neglect the present and forget about the future.
- Passion (*raja guṇa*), which pushes us to neglect the past, overlook the present and obsess with the future;
- Goodness (*sattva guṇa*), which leads us to learn from the past and prepare for the future by acting thoughtfully in the present.

Expanding the influence of *sattva guṇa* in our lives opens the door for a pleasurable inner life of ongoing spiritual bliss and realization. For this reason, Grandfather Bhīṣma advised Yudhiṣṭhir to train his citizens for a life of goodness in these nine ways:

- Control anger. Learn to recognize and acknowledge hostility without indulging in expressing it on the spot.
- Always tell the truth. With allowances for diplomacy, this policy makes life simple and keeps the conscience clear.
- Be charitable. It is not true that, "Whoever dies with the most toys wins."
- Tolerate others. More on this in Chapter 10.
- Be faithful in marriage. This is easiest for God conscious partners.
- Be clean, mentally and physically. A daily bath, simple foods and exercise keep the body clean. Doing daily meditation and revealing our thoughts to trusted confidantes helps purify the mind.
- Be kind. Positive relationships satisfy us more than material things.
- Be simple. Real wealth is having all you need.
- Take good care of dependents. Be a servant-leader for children, students and employees.

Living in the mode of goodness reduces the distractions of materialistic life. When we choose goodness, we gain the ability to focus on spirituality, freed from old habits of pondering the past (ignorance) or fretting over the future (passion). As explained in Chapter One, text 34, at that point our minds can become receptive to and deeply enlivened by higher knowledge of the Supreme.

> As lust, desire and greediness are swept out of the way,
> you move ahead to goodness and great happiness each day.
> In touch with pure devotion and relieved of low desire,
> immersed in Krishna science, you'll be thoroughly inspired.
> You'll pierce the knot of false attachment, elevate your soul,
> and end the chain of karma as your faith takes solid hold.

Bhīṣma embodies this rise through the modes. This great bhakta was caught up in political obligations that forced him to fight against his beloved nephews the Pandavas, as well as his revered Lord Krishna. Duryodhana, Bhīṣma's manipulative boss and nephew, kept pushing him to kill Arjuna, the Pandava's best warrior. Bhīṣma vowed to either kill Arjuna or force Lord Krishna to break His vow not to fight in the great battle.

As they fought, Arjuna and Bhīṣma were equally matched, and Arjuna could not bring himself to fire his arrows at full strength against his aged, beloved uncle. As Bhīṣma gained the upper hand, Krishna jumped from Arjuna's chariot, which He had been driving in a non-combat role. He grabbed a broken chariot wheel lying nearby and rushed at Bhīṣma. Seeing this, Bhīṣma gladly readied himself to die at Krishna's hand and end his painful obligations in the war. However, the sun set just at that moment, signaling the end of the day's fighting.

Later, mortally wounded by Arjuna, with the war over and no longer possessed of the passion and political views a warrior requires, Bhīṣma turned to goodness, instructing the Pandava King Yudhiṣṭhir about how to lead citizens to happy, moral lives. Bhīṣma then entered full spiritual meditation, remembering Lord Krishna on the battlefield as well as His more intimate relationships with the cowherd girls of Vraj, the rural land where Krishna grew up. His mind peacefully absorbed in Krishna, Bhīṣma gave up his body and returned to the spiritual world.

SIX

BHAKTAS

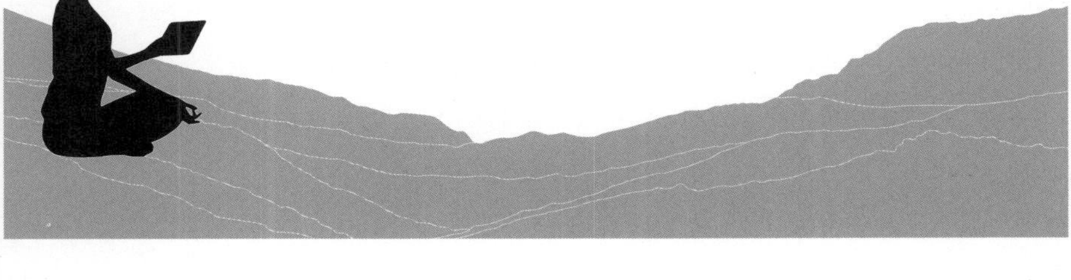

KRISHNA LEAVES HASTINĀPUR (1-13)

And how, you ask, did Yudhiṣṭhir give up or set aside
the guilt he had been feeling since so many men had died?
Both Bhīṣma and Lord Krishna helped relieve his great remorse,
so he and his four brothers put the kingdom back on course.

The wise and pious Yudhiṣṭhir spread such a godly mood
that ample rains began to fall and earth produced more food.
So happy were the cows protected by his righteous shield
that milk from their abundant udders soaked the grazing fields.

The rivers quenched the farmer's fields and oceans yielded jewels.
The forests offered fruits and herbs and wood to use for fuel.
Because they loved King Yudhiṣṭhir, who had no one to fear,
the citizens felt fit and calm. Their troubles disappeared.

Once Krishna had helped Yudhiṣṭhir to ease the hearts aggrieved
by losses in the battle, He declared it time to leave.
He took permission from the King, bowed low before the throne,
and climbed aboard His chariot for Dvārakā, His home.

Since sages grow attached to Krishna hearing these narrations,
could those who saw Him daily tolerate His separation?
While Krishna was preparing to depart that very day,
the royalty who loved Him nearly fainted dead away.

Observing Krishna closely with unblinking, anxious stares,
the palace residents were stunned and wandered here and there.
A flock of ladies dashed to see Him, sad and thunderstruck,
attempting not to cry, for that provoked unpleasant luck.
With shyness and with admiration, from the palace roof,
the ladies showered flowers on their Lord, yet stayed aloof.

As He left Hastināpur, people shouted Krishna's name
with conch shells, cymbals, drums and more in blissful serenade.

Absorbed in thought of Krishna, all the ordinary men
exalted Him in poetry as sweet as Vedic hymns.
While climbing to their rooftops to extend their fond farewells,
the Hastināpur ladies whispered thus among themselves:

"Oh, there goes Krishna, God Himself, the shelter of us all.
He makes this world of matter for we spirit souls who fall.
But great devotees, free of sin and all mundane desire
can go again to Krishna when their mortal lives expire.

The Vedas praise Lord Krishna and His great activities.
He spins out giant planets then withdraws them all with ease.
When beastly men disguised as kings take charge, the Lord descends
to vanquish them in different ways while rescuing His friends.

How blessed is Mathurā, for Krishna played there as a boy.
How blessed are the Yadus, for He brings their kingdom joy.
And Dvārakā, His capital, makes heaven appear vile,
for all of its inhabitants can see His pleasing smile.

Lord Krishna's queens in Dvārakā, though sought by lesser men,
fulfilled their deepest heart's desire when they were wed to Him.
Just how were they so privileged to gain His loving kiss?
The very thought makes gopis in Vṛndāvan faint in bliss."

On hearing these enchanting words, Lord Krishna glanced and smiled
while leaving Hastināpur for His queens and domicile.
Though Yudhiṣṭhir and others walked with Him a long, long way,
at last the Lord convinced them they were duty-bound to stay.

KRISHNA REACHES DVĀRAKĀ (14-34)

Lord Krishna entered Dvārakā and blew His conch aloud.
The residents rejoiced as if the sound had lifted clouds.
His white, enormous conch shell, tinged with red where Krishna blew,
resembled a white swan at play in crimson lotus blooms.

The sound of Krishna's conch shell made the people so inspired,
they ran to have His audience, which they had long desired.
When they gave gifts to Krishna, who looks after everyone,
they looked like priests who offer tiny candles to the sun.

The people said, "Our dear Lord Krishna, gods declare Your praise.
Your very form is endless truth that time cannot decay.
Our Father, Mother, Guru, God! By following Your trail,
we all feel blessed and meet success in every detail.

The moments turn to centuries whenever You're away,
for we feel stuck in darkest night without the hope of day.
Now once again Your charming smile has quieted our fear,
and gods in heaven envy us for having You so near.

Dear Krishna, when You go away and we don't see You smile,
who else can ease our suffering and make our lives worthwhile?"
On seeing Krishna glance at them and feeling reassured,
the people praised His presence with cascades of pleasing words.

The city, kissed by shining sun and gentle springtime showers,
displayed her gardens, orchards, parks and lakes with lotus flowers.
Fresh mango and banana leaves adorned the promenade,
where garlands, flags and painted banners all provided shade.

The people cleansed the lanes and grounds with water and perfume,
and everywhere were fruits and grains and flowers freshly bloomed.
To welcome back Lord Krishna, each and every house displayed
sweet incense, water, fruits and yogurt, set on gleaming trays.

On learning of the Lord's return, the royal family
rose up from rest or dining and departed hurriedly.
With elephants and bugle blasts, they rode on royal carts.
As learned priests recited hymns, affection filled their hearts.

The actors, singers, artists, and the scribes of history
all celebrated Krishna, each by their ability.
And even well-known prostitutes, the victims of ill chance,
came out to see the Lord arrive, their beauty much enhanced.

Lord Krishna offered due respect to everyone who came
and greeted both the common folk and those of royal fame.
He bowed His head, shook hands, embraced and gave His heartfelt thanks
to bless and reassure them all, regardless of their rank.

The senior priests and relatives praised Krishna loud and long,
and everyone exalted Him with thunderous, blissful song.
Observing from their palace roofs, the ladies were amazed
as Krishna turned the morning to a festive holiday.

The citizens of Dvārakā saw Krishna frequently,
and yet they never missed a single opportunity.
His lotus feet are havens and His face the source of charm,
and fortune's Queen adorns His chest, the gods His sturdy arms.

Lord Krishna's face, the color of the clouds of the monsoon,
was shaded by umbrellas shaped like flaxen autumn moons.
It shone among His garlands strung in gorgeous rainbow stripes
upon His yellow silken dress that flashed like lightning strikes.

On entering His father's house, the Lord was pleased to see
His father's many wives and His own mother, Devakī.
The ladies all embraced their son as milk enlarged their breasts,
and when He sat upon their laps, their tears came forth unchecked.

Thereafter, Krishna left for His palatial private homes.
In each one lived a wife convinced the Lord was hers alone.
By wondrous mystic power, Krishna managed to expand
for sixteen thousand palace queens who each sought out His hand.

His queens came running forth to Him, rejoicing in their minds,
for He had been away from them for quite a lengthy time.
Within their hearts they held Him, though in public they were shy,
and as they sent their sons to greet Him, tears adorned their eyes.

Lord Krishna stayed close by His wives, as any husband should,
and they did not grow tired of Him, as common spouses would,
for even Laxmi, Queen of wealth, whose restlessness is famed,
will always stay at Krishna's feet. Could any woman stray?

Lord Krishna felt at peace after the Kurukṣetra war,
for armies that had burdened Earth could trouble her no more.
As rubbing bamboo branches can ignite a forest fire,
the Lord made armies kill each other, filling Earth's desire,

At home at last among His wives, He seemed a common man,
though Krishna does so many things that only Krishna can.
A single Queen could turn Lord Śiva's rock-hard vows to dust,
yet all His Queens together could not conjure Krishna's lust.

A worldly soul imagines that the Lord is just like him,
and suffers from attachments and desires He cannot stem.
Though Krishna does encounter matter, He remains divine,
as do all those who follow Him with loving, steadfast minds.

Lord Krishna's wives, divinely tricked, could only think of Him
as their beloved husband, not the goal of Vedic hymns.
Like atheists who can't see God, these rare, devoted souls
could not imagine God could be a husband they controlled.

STRATEGY #6: SERVE WITHOUT STIPULATION

Throughout this section of the *Bhāgavat Purāṇa*, many bhaktas beg Krishna to stay with them. At their request He would sometimes postpone other plans and stay, but usually only for a short time. Clearly, Krishna knew they would be fine without Him around. How could He be so sure?

Krishna, who resides in everyone's heart, understands the feelings of advanced bhaktas who share a loving relationship with Him. Compare their service mood with that of atheists and beginning bhaktas. Atheists insist that God show Himself so they can decide whether or not to do Him a big favor by believing in Him. Similarly, novices may try bhakti for some time only to quit when Krishna doesn't magically show up. Such bhakti is conditional: "If the Supreme proves Himself, I'll continue. Otherwise, forget it."

Imagine how this looks from Krishna's point of view. His only intention is to help us. Would it really help us for the Supreme to reveal Himself so we can think about having a relationship with Him? Would it be wise for Him to indulge our every unearned, undeserved wish, like parents of a spoiled child, without instilling in us the self-discipline to go through the rigors of life? An old story illustrates this point.

After a young boy's parents died, his aunt adopted and raised him. But because she felt sorry for her orphaned nephew, she could never bring herself to punish him. As a result of growing up without any discipline, he became a criminal. Eventually he committed a murder and was sentenced to be hanged. Bound and standing on the scaffold, he requested a final word with his aunt. As she walked towards him tearfully, he beckoned her to come closer and closer, as if to whisper something to her. But to her horror, when she put her ear to his mouth, he violently bit it and snarled, "If you had disciplined me, I wouldn't be here now."

This bitter tale demonstrates that real love does not mean catering to the beloved's every demand. Of course, a giving spirit is good, but it should be mutual. If one person gives and the other only takes, is that love or exploitation? We should not try to exploit the Supreme, seeing Him as our order supplier. It is said, "First deserve, then desire."

One who puts in no effort but arrogantly demands the Supreme to appear will eventually see the Supreme, not in His beautiful form of Krishna but in His form of Time which ultimately destroys everyone and everything. On the other hand, deserving bhaktas who do their part in the relationship will begin to see the Supreme in His more lovable form, a consistently sweet vision reserved for those with loving eyes.

As the great bhakti teacher Bhaktisiddhanta Sarasvati Thakur put it, "Don't try to see God; try to act in such a way that God sees you." This is the attitude of advanced bhaktas.

In fact, when Krishna is absent, the love of advanced bhaktas increases. This is natural in genuine relationships. As the poet Bayly wrote:

"What would not I give to wander
Where my old companions dwell?
Absence makes the heart grow fonder;
Isle of Beauty, fare thee well!"

Whether we know it or not, we have a permanent loving relationship with our maker, and He misses us more than we miss Him. In the *Bhagavad-gītā* 18.65 He says that through bhakti we will come to see Him, concluding with the Sanskrit words *pratijāne priyso 'si me*: "I promise you this because you are My very dear friend."

In this chapter we see that Yudhiṣṭhir's deep love for Krishna influenced his subjects to love Krishna too, so much so that they could not bear the idea of Him leaving. Yet Krishna did leave them, knowing that the pain of separation would be a great incentive for them to remember and serve Him. For one feeling separation from the Supreme, thoughtful spiritual service becomes the only solace. Thus, Krishna left Yudhiṣṭhir and his subjects knowing that their spiritual lives would be improved.

On the other end of Krishna's journey, the residents of Dvārakā, including His many wives and children, were overjoyed to see Him again. If Krishna hadn't left, they could never have experienced this bliss of reunion. Prince, princess or prostitute, no one was left out. Regardless of their place in society, when Krishna arrived, all of these special souls enjoyed a unique loving reciprocation.

For a bhakta, there is joy both in union with and separation from the Supreme. Krishna may or may not be present, but the bhakta's connection remains constant through service. Compare that mood with self-centered meditation intended to make the meditator one with the Supreme. Loving service to the Supreme goes on perpetually, in any situation, with Him or without Him, as shown by the great bhaktas in this chapter.

SEVEN

YUDHIṢṬHIR

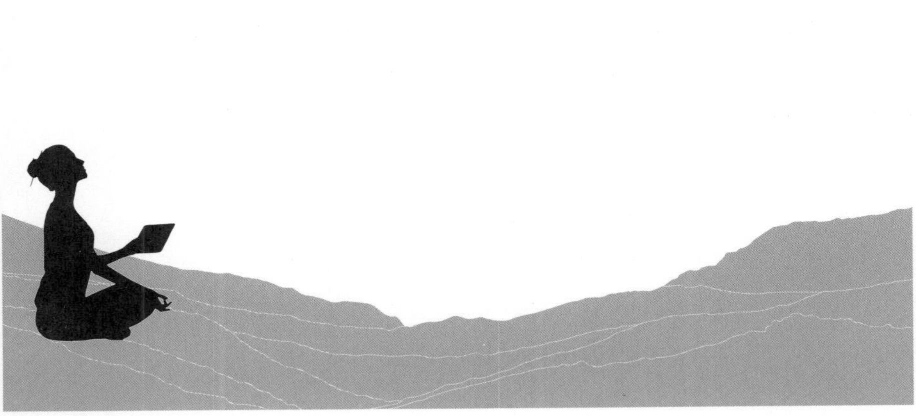

VIṢṆURĀTA SAVED IN THE WOMB (1-7)

You now have heard how Krishna helped to settle Yudhiṣṭhir,
and then returned to Dvārakā, where people held Him dear,
Let's now discuss the embryo within Uttarā's womb,
King Yudhiṣṭhir's successor, as was generally assumed.

Do you recall how Krishna saved the unborn little boy
when Aśvattāmā, son of Droṇa, angrily deployed
the great brahmāstra weapon, which can devastate the Earth?
The child thus saw Lord Krishna's beauty well before his birth.

Bound up inside Uttarā's womb, the child felt brutal heat,
a sign of the brahmāstra, which no mortal could defeat.
And then he saw the Lord appear, no larger than a thumb.
On seeing this enchanting sight, the child was overcome.

With robes of yellow silk and golden helmet on His head,
the Lord looked quite appealing, though His eyes were fury-red.
His club in hand, He vanquished the brahmāstra's deadly hue
as easily as morning sunlight dries a drop of dew.

Lord Krishna, God, is everywhere, unchecked by time or space.
He always saves the righteous and puts sinners in their place.
Defusing the brahmāstra in the presence of the child,
the Lord then disappeared and left the tiny boy beguiled.

In time, the stars and planets shifted to auspicious signs
and ushered to this world the heir of Pāṇḍu's royal line.
The vigilant King Yudhiṣṭhir observed this with delight,
and called the royal priests to execute the proper rites.

In honor of the newborn boy, King Yudhiṣṭhir released
much gold and land and other wealth to suit the royal priests.
Content with Yudhiṣṭhir, his gifts, and all that had occurred,
the priests extolled his heritage and grandson with these words:

PROPHECIES FOR THE CHILD (8-19)

"The timing of this infant's birth has very clearly shown
that God has sent a spotless child to grace King Pāṇḍu's throne.
Lord Krishna saved him in the womb, so let the prince be known
as Viṣṇurāta, one whose life depends on God alone."

Said Yudhiṣṭhir, "Oh best of those who know astrology,
will this child guard religion and yet rule effectively?
Will he be as accomplished and as famous in his time
as all his predecessors in King Pāṇḍu's royal line?"

The priests replied, "When he is king, this child shall be acclaimed
for guarding man and beast alike who live within his reign.
Like mighty Ram, who left his throne to fill his father's vow,
where this child rules, deceitfulness will never be allowed.

In days gone by, the great King Śibi saved a helpless bird.
An eagle had it cornered, but King Śibi gave his word
to substitute his own flesh to the eagle's hungry beak.
This child shall likewise grant complete protection for the weak.

In shooting arrows, he shall match Arjuna. He shall be
compelling like a forest fire and forceful like the sea.
With lion-strength he'll answer any troubled person's call,
just as the Himālayan range can shelter one and all.

Forbearing as the earth and fair in mind as you, O King,
this child, like generous Śiva, will give people everything.
The citizens shall flock to him for safety, hope and health
as people flock to Krishna, even Śrī, the queen of wealth.

King Rantidev, a saintly soul, had fasted forty days,
but gave away his break-fast meal to guests who came his way.
This child shall match King Rantidev in magnanimity
and nearly equal Krishna in such godly qualities.

In patience he'll match Bali, who, despite his guru's pleas,
presented to Lord Krishna all the planets he had seized.
In staunch determination he will equal young Prahlād,
whose father tried to kill him for promoting love of God.

Protecting peace on earth, he will rebuke offensive men.
His children will be glorious and saintly, just like him.
Though knowing of his death well in advance, he won't protest.
Instead, he'll turn to Krishna and renounce his royal dress.
The learned Śukadev shall guide him through this fatal strife,
and help him find Lord Krishna and fulfill his goal in life."

King Yudhiṣṭhir heard all of this, and feeling very pleased,
he blessed the court astrologers with all necessities.
He pictured Viṣṇurāta growing like the waxing moon
and seeking out Lord Krishna, whom he'd seen while in the womb.

To celebrate the prince's birth and clear away the sin
of Kurukṣetra's battle, which destroyed so many men,
King Yudhiṣṭhir performed a costly Vedic sacrifice,
as Bhīṣma and Lord Krishna had repeatedly advised.

STRATEGY #7: LOOK AHEAD

Here we see King Yudhiṣṭhir consulting learned astrologers who make a glorious prediction about the newborn child's character and future. Apparently, at that time, such predictions were accurate and considered so important that the kings would often turn to their palace priests for astrological advice.

What about astrology these days? How seriously should we take it? The prospect of seeing the future through astrology fascinates nearly everyone. Some look at their astrological charts with passing interest and then forget about them. Others check the stars each morning before stepping out the door.

Even if we take astrology seriously, it is important to keep perspective. When a questioner once asked Śrila Prabhupada to predict his future, Śrila Prabhupada smiled and replied, "You will grow old and die." This blanket horoscope may seem like a no-brainer. But it points to an important fact which most of us prefer to ignore: whatever success we may find in family, finance, romance and career will all be taken away sooner or later.

Depressing? If these things are all that we're living for, maybe. Fortunately, there's much more to be achieved in life. According to the Vedic literatures, the whole purpose of human life is to advance spiritually. And here's a switch: as soon as we wholeheartedly take to spiritual life, our destiny changes, making our astrological forecast largely irrelevant. That one choice—to go for spiritual rather than material goals—changes the whole game.

Spiritual life or ordinary life? It's a difficult choice for most of us, yet remaining undecided can also hurt us. Indecision subtly creates a gnawing, persistent anxiety in our lives, stressing us and leading to gross, self-defeating behaviors as we desperately seek a little peace. An existential anxiety resulting from unsettled spirituality can apply just as much to the materially successful as it does to the underprivileged. We need to make a choice.

Yudhiṣṭhir, a committed spiritualist, suffered many setbacks yet remained peaceful within. After much difficulty he has filled his external duties as well. In this chapter of the *Bhāgavat Purāṇa* we see him in a joyful mood, having a competent heir to take over his position. That frees him to retire as king and fully devote himself to self-realization through bhakti-yoga.

Yudhiṣṭhir's attitude is in stark contrast to that of modern leaders who, ignorant of the spiritual side of life, struggle to hang on to power until the last possible moment. Little do they know that real happiness comes from spiritual life. If our material life is going well but our spiritual life is not, we are subject to disruption at any moment. On the other hand, if our spiritual life is going well, we can be happy even in great external difficulty.

Yudhiṣṭhir knows all this, so as a responsible king, he first checks with competent astrologers to make sure that his duties will be covered. He then turns his full attention to inner development. At this point in Yudhiṣṭhir's own life, there is little need for horoscope readings, for a life of devotion to the Supreme is beyond the purview of astrology and directly managed by the personal hand of the Supreme.

EIGHT

DHṚTARĀṢṬRA

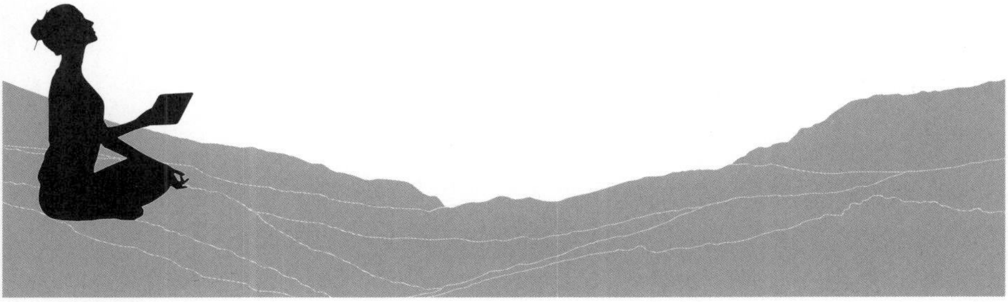

VIDURA RETURNS (1-11)

Now let us all go back in time, before the fateful war
when Pāṇḍu ruled the kingdom and was generally adored.
His older brother Dhṛtarāṣṭra would have had his place.
He was inclined, but being blind he could not lead his race.

A third brother, Vidura, who was youngest of the three
could not become the king because his mom was not a queen.
The sons of Dhṛtarāṣṭra snatched the throne when Pāṇḍu died,
but Pāṇḍu's sons recovered it, with Krishna at their side.

Ignoring family battles, wise Vidura kept his head,
and left the lavish palace for a pilgrim's humble bed.
In classic Vedic fashion, he attended holy sites,
awakening devotion and his spiritual delight.

The civil war completed and the Pāṇḍavas enthroned,
Vidura, in his wisdom, finally made his way back home.
Queen Kuntī, Dhṛtarāṣṭra, the five Pāṇḍavas and all
rejoiced to greet Vidura when he reached the palace hall.

The family members all agreed Vidura gave them strength
as they embraced him feelingly and praised him at some length.
King Yudhiṣṭhir at once arranged Vidura's food and rest,
then seated him with everyone and asked his honored guest,

"Our dear Uncle Vidura, I recall your caring arms
protecting us from poison and a deadly fire's harm.
While traveling, how did you cope and care for life and limb?
What sites of God did you attend, and how did you serve Him?

A man like you makes any place seem sacred, pure and bright.
It seems by Krishna's grace you are a walking holy site.
Now, did you go to Dvārakā, where Krishna's family
remains absorbed in thoughts of Him in loving ecstasy?"

Vidura then pleased everyone by telling of his tour
and how he met Maitreya, whose instructions made him pure.
He answered every question raised by Yudhiṣṭhir that day,
except of Dvārakā and Krishna's family and their fate.

Vidura couldn't bear to pain his nephew's smiling face
recounting the disasters that he knew had taken place.
"They'll learn about it soon enough," the wise Vidura mused.
"Why should I spoil their happiness disclosing dreadful news?"

Although he had renounced the world and had no needs at all,
Vidura stayed there with his kin within the palace walls.
His nephews asked for guidance and he answered them in kind,
though it was Dhṛtarāṣṭra that Vidura had in mind.

Vidura knew his other work did not demand his time.
He knew the reign of Yudhiṣṭhir would surely be sublime.
He also knew how time creeps up and wholly overwhelms
a soul engrossed in family life who thinks of nothing else.

A SECRET CONFRONTATION (12-21)

And so Vidura went to see his brother late one day.
He whispered, "Dhṛtarāṣṭra, you must leave without delay,
for Krishna in His form of Time has caught you indisposed
and living at the mercy of your slaughtered children's foes.

Your father, brother, well-wishers and sons are all now dead.
You're unprepared to meet your death, with little time ahead.
You're blind, you'll soon be deaf, and now your memory is off.
Your teeth are loose, your liver's bad, and day and night you cough.

How forceful are the hopes of one attached to home and wife.
How much he'll bow and shame himself to save his wretched life.
You've grown to be the palace dog who grovels, sits and comes
to eat the scraps of Bhīma, who destroyed your hundred sons.

Though Yudhiṣṭhir is right to care and see that you're maintained,
for you to take his endless help should make you feel ashamed.
Remember, you tried killing him with poison and with fire
and stole away his kingdom to appease your son's desire?

Despite your plan to carry on, at cost of pride and fame,
your body, like a rotting shirt, grows ever weak and lame.
Now, can you understand the truth by looking at yourself,
or do you need to be awakened by somebody else?

The brutal truth, my brother, is that death comes ever near.
The self-controlled leave home to die, detached and free of fear.
Such people see the misery that birth and death impart
and give up sense enjoyment, finding God within the heart.

Now please, my learned brother, like an ancient Vedic sage,
before you are bewildered by the coming Kali age,
go northward to the mountains. Leave the palace right away.
Do not inform your relatives; they'll only block your way."

Old Dhṛtarāṣṭra drew his breath. The shock of what he'd heard
confounded him at first, but he accepted every word.
Resolving in an instant to cut off his family ties,
he walked out of the palace with Vidura as his guide.

Now Dhṛtarāṣṭra's wife Gāndhārī quickly understood
that he would end his life as an ascetic in the woods.
Because of her great chastity, she left home with him, too,
and vowed to linger at his side until his life was through.

Gāndhārī went at her own risk; she knew her husband swore
that he would not concern himself with loved ones any more.
Gāndhārī joined the brothers walking north throughout the night
like honored soldiers battle-scarred from long and worthy fight.

A SHOCKING DISCOVERY (22-27)

The sun arose as Yudhiṣṭhir, the saint among the kings,
began his day as usual with prayers and offerings.
He worshipped all the royal priests with gifts of gold and land,
and went to show respects to all the elders of his clan.

The palace servant told the king, with numb and vacant stare,
that Dhṛtarāṣṭra and Vidura were no longer there.
Gāndhārī, too, was missing. Yudhiṣṭhir was shocked. And then,
he saw Sañjaya, Dhṛtarāṣṭra's aide, and cried to him,

"Where is the great Vidura who allays my troubled mind?
Where is our revered uncle, who is elderly and blind?
His wife and he have lost their sons. I gave them no relief.
Have they entered the river just to drown and end their grief?"

Sañjaya could not answer. Sorrow paralyzed his tongue.
He served old Dhṛtarāṣṭra long and well. He too was stunned.
Not knowing how Vidura had inspired his master's heart,
Sañjaya, too, thought grief had led the elders to depart.

Sañjaya then composed himself, brushed off his teary eyes,
and thought of Dhṛtarāṣṭra as he offered this reply:

"Dear scion of the Kurus, in this gray and empty dawn,
I do not know where Dhṛtarāṣṭra and his wife have gone.
They did not say a word to me before they chose to go.
You see, I too am cheated by those great, exalted souls."

UNEXPECTED HELP (28-41)

As all despaired and sat in shock, expressing many fears,
the ever-traveling Nārada surprisingly appeared.
He played upon his vina and displayed a lustrous gleam.
King Yudhiṣṭhir and everyone stood up to show esteem.

"Oh godly sage," cried Yudhiṣṭhir, "my uncles fled our door,
along with my unblemished aunt, who lost her sons in war.
They left us all adrift upon an ocean of remorse.
Can you direct our ship, dear sage, and put us back on course?"

Said Nārada, "A righteous king has nothing to bemoan,
for everybody's actions are controlled by God alone.
Though men think they assemble to extol the Lord in verse,
the Lord in fact assembles them and then makes them disperse.
Like cows attached to nose rings on a strong and lengthy cord,
we all are bound completely to the wishes of the Lord.

As players set out pawns and later put them all away,
the Lord alone determines who will go and who will stay.

Do you suppose the body is the greatest human prize,
or do you think the soul continues when the body dies?
And even if the soul and flesh were somehow intertwined,
are bodily affections not illusions of your mind?

You think that you are young and strong and feel yourself compelled
to care for helpless elders and make sure that they are well.
A serpent grips your body; how can you look after theirs
when nature, time and karma rule your bodily affairs?

Those creatures who possess no hands are prey for those who do,
and creatures who can walk about eat sedentary food.
Since every living being somehow lives upon another,
you really needn't worry for your uncle and his brother.

The Lord is anywhere your aunt and uncles may have gone,
so look to Him to care for them so you can carry on.
Lord Krishna has descended as indomitable time
to rid the world of demons for the good of humankind.

Lord Krishna has His purpose, so you've nothing left to fear.
Remain here with your brothers until Krishna disappears.
Your aged aunt and uncles will soon reach the southern side
of Himālaya's mountains, where the saintly souls reside.

While sitting by the Gaṅgā, Dhṛtarāṣṭra will engage
in eight-fold yoga practice, taking bath three times a day.
By executing fire rites while on a water fast,
he'll conquer all his senses and forget about his past.

Performing yoga postures as he learns to rule his breath,
he'll see he's not his body and prepare himself for death.
Refining his intelligence with godly qualities,
at last he'll come to realize his true identity.

Impervious to worldly cares and all contamination,
he'll undertake an absolute, unbroken meditation.
He'll thoroughly detach himself within a few more days.
His flesh will then incinerate by force of mystic blaze.

Gāndhārī shall prefer a fire to painful separation,
and share in Dhṛtarāṣṭra's pyre as well as his salvation.
Vidura, feeling joy and grief to see the bodies burn,
shall leave again for pilgrimage and nevermore return."

Assuring Yudhiṣṭhir that he had filled his obligations,
Saint Nārada relieved the king of all his lamentation.
King Yudhiṣṭhir, astonished, took these prophecies to heart,
as Nārada, his purpose filled, proceeded to depart.

STRATEGY #8: GET REAL

Dhṛtarāṣṭra was blind from birth, yet worse than his physical disability was his lack of spiritual vision. Although it was against the interests of his own kingdom, he consistently gave in to his son's plans to cheat and even murder the Pandavas, who were led by the righteous Yudhiṣṭhir. After the ensuing war, when all his sons were dead, Dhṛtarāṣṭra shamelessly remained in the royal comfort of Yudhiṣṭhir's palace. The saintly Yudhiṣṭhir loved and honored his aged uncle, while the wise Vidura saw his brother Dhṛtarāṣṭra's situation as pathetic. So Vidura secretly confronted Dhṛtarāṣṭra and convinced him to overcome his spiritual inertia and act honorably.

Like Dhṛtarāṣṭra , we too often remain stuck in problematic situations. Why? Have we grown accustomed to discomfort? Do we see no alternative? Are we too lazy to change?

One such predicament that affects us all is being stuck in a material body. As eternal souls in temporary bodies, we live in an inherently incompatible and problematic situation. The body deteriorates, bringing pain and disappointment. Faculties we take for granted—seeing, hearing, digesting and thinking, using our arms and legs, as well as having the energy to take on new tasks and adventures—any or all of these assets can be lost at any time. Everyone knows this, yet within, we instinctively feel entitled to be healthy and young. Why?

As souls, we are always healthy and young. The *Bhagavad-gītā* describes the soul as unchangeable and indestructible, full of endless bliss and wisdom. However, due to misidentifying with the material body, the person within undergoes endless problems. The practice of bhakti-yoga frees one from this illusion. One practicing bhakti gets real about both the material

body and spiritual opportunity. This frank look at reality unlocks an inner enjoyment that is independent of any physical condition.
Vidura specifically points out to Dhṛtarāṣṭra that his aging body is a clear sign that death is approaching. "You're losing your teeth, your hearing and your liver," he told him. "Instead of wallowing in palace luxury, now is the time for self-realization." Vidura was speaking from personal experience. He himself had left the palace years before, giving up royal comforts for the sake of integrity and spiritual advancement. Now, meeting again late in their lives, the two brothers' positions are vastly different. Dhṛtarāṣṭra, languishing in the palace, thinks only of himself. He struggles to forget his painful past and to ignore the frightening future. By contrast, Vidura, empowered and well-adjusted with spiritual realization, finds compassion and helps his bewildered brother.

Vidura's kindness again demonstrates the importance of spiritual mentors. As Dhṛtarāṣṭra hovers on the verge of an entirely wasted life, Vidura rescues him. Then, as Yudhiṣṭhir is overcome with grief, Nārada reassures him, prophetically reminding him that his situation, like Dhṛtarāṣṭra's, cannot last.

We all need a mentor in spiritual life, but we should be careful to accept one that is genuinely going to help us. While self-centered, manipulative "mentors" tend to flatter and exploit us, true well-wishers, like Vidura, kick our butts and help us get real.

NINE

ARJUNA

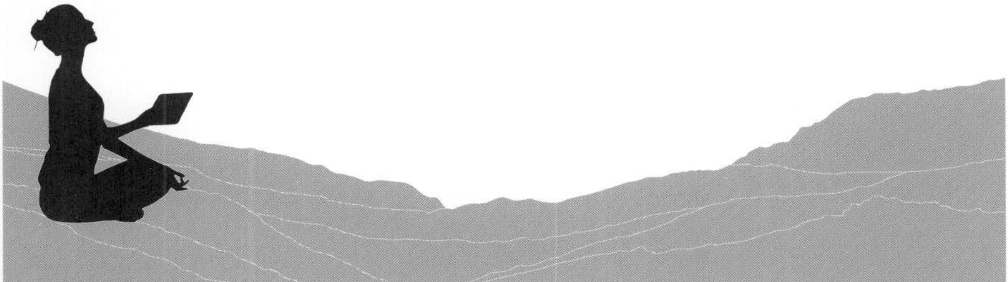

EVIL OMENS HAUNT YUDHIṢṬHIRA (1-16)

King Yudhiṣṭhir remembered how Lord Krishna eased the weight
imposed upon the earth by kings possessed of greed and hate.
Arjuna went to Dvārakā to learn of Krishna's plans,
so Yudhiṣṭhir could wisely meet the monarchy's demands.

Arjuna traveled westward to that kingdom by the sea,
to meet the Lord and others of the Yadu dynasty.
A string of evil omens then made Yudhiṣṭhir concerned
and left him still more anxious for his brother to return.

Just after Yudhiṣṭhir dispatched his trusted younger brother,
the weather due in one season turned up within another.
Good citizens transformed into a greedy, angry mob
and cheated for their livelihood, neglecting honest jobs.

Beloved, trusted friends began to cheat on one another,
and quarrels manifested between fathers, sons and mothers.
Pernicious disagreements broke the bonds of man and wife.
King Yudhiṣṭhir had never seen his subjects in such strife.

As citizens degraded to unrighteous, troubled ways,
King Yudhiṣṭhir began to wonder where he'd gone astray.
While thinking his reign pious and this trouble undeserved,
he called his brother Bhīma to his chambers and observed;

"Arjuna went for Krishna's counsel. Seven months have passed,
and in his absence many evil omens have amassed.
I wonder if Lord Krishna has departed from our lives
as Nārada predicted. Has the time so soon arrived?

Lord Krishna has delivered us a kingdom rich with gold,
our wives, our heir, our triumphs and imperial control.
It's only due to Krishna that we draw our very breath,
and only by His grace can we go forward after death.

Just see, my mighty brother, how these threefold miseries,
produced of one's own flesh, one's peers, or higher deities,
alert us all repeatedly of dangers yet to come.
Yet we proceed as usual. How foolish we've become.

The left side of my body, for what seems like many days,
has constantly been trembling in an inauspicious way.
My heart is palpitating due to vague, uneasy fear.
These signs imply an evil time is quickly drawing near.

The jackal-bitch rebukes the moon while spewing acrid flame,
and barking dogs harass me without fear, respect or shame.
A donkey walks around me, while my horse appears bereft.
Auspicious beasts like cows now pass me only on my left.

Just see! The pigeon heralds news of detriment and doom,
while shrieking owls and ravens fill my heart with dread and gloom.
These birds foretell the world collapsing in some great abyss.
O Bhīma, have you ever seen such inauspiciousness?

The earth and mountains throb beneath an evil, smoky sky,
while lightning bolts from cloudless thunder shock and mystify.
When clouds do come, they shower blood in terrible monsoons,
as violent winds hurl dust about and dim the sky at noon.

The sun recedes quite early, turning evening into night,
revealing stars that seem engaged in bitter, vicious fights.

I'm not the only one who holds such pessimistic views,
for everyone I see is shedding tears and quite confused.

The rivers, lakes and reservoirs rise ominously higher,
and ghee no longer sets ablaze the sacrificial fire.
My mind is weak and seems to grow increasingly disturbed.
What is this strange, perplexing time, and what is to occur?

The cows no longer nurse their calves. They cry all day and night.
The bulls out in the pastures can no longer find delight.
The Deities appear to weep and want to leave Their shrines.
Our lovely towns are ugly now. Is this the end of time?

These dreadful omens indicate some great catastrophe
will soon descend and put an end to earth's tranquility.
Although the touch of Krishna's feet made planet Earth feel graced,
these signs warn of a coming time when Earth will be debased."

A SHATTERED ARJUNA RETURNS (17-39)

As Yudhiṣṭhir expressed his fears to Bhīma in this way,
it happened that Arjuna came back home that very day.
As his great brother walked to him, King Yudhiṣṭhir surmised
Arjuna was consumed with grief, for tears obscured his eyes.

The King was shocked to see Arjuna sickly, weak and pale.
"The prophecies of Nārada," he thought, "shall never fail."

As many friends arrived and sensed the dread within the room,
the King inquired of Arjuna that fateful afternoon:

"Dear brother, welcome home! You look so tired. Did you spend
a pleasant time in Dvārakā among our Yadu friends?
And how is Vasudeva and his seven sister-brides,
the eldest of whom, Devakī, is always at his side?"

King Yudhiṣṭhir remembered many leading Yadu names,
inquiring of their welfare and the state of their domains.

And then the King continued, "What of Krishna? How is He
who loves the cows, the brahmans and His faithful devotees?
Since Krishna and his brother grace their kingdom by the sea,
these must be days of pleasure for the Yadu dynasty."

King Yudhiṣṭhir asked further of Lord Krishna's friends and wives.
but all could see Arjuna didn't meet his brother's eyes.
At last the King inquired, "Dear Arjuna, are you sick?
Did somebody mistreat you as you made your lengthy trip?

Did someone speak unkindly words or dare to threaten you?
Could you not give in charity or pay some sort of dues?
You always guard the cows, the priests, the women and the weak.
Have you now disappointed them? Arjuna, can you speak?

Did you approach a woman of uncertain quality
or leave a more deserving woman with indignity?
Has some unworthy enemy picked up a sword and shield
and beaten you in combat on some distant battlefield?

Did you neglect to give some children necessary food
or disregard some older men who should have dined with you?
As you returned from Dvārakā and tired on the way
did you by chance perform some great, unspeakable mistake?

Or could it be you seem so bleak because you've been deprived
of your most confidential friend, authority and guide?
Has Krishna gone away, Arjuna? I cannot conceive
of any other reason why you sit so still and grieve."

ARJUNA'S LAMENT (27-40)

Arjuna barely heard the King spell out his speculations
for he was numb and dumbstruck from Lord Krishna's separation.
His handsome mouth and fluid heart appeared to have gone dry.
His body pale, Arjuna failed to utter a reply.

Arjuna smeared his hands across his reddened, teary eyes
and thought of Krishna's love as he released a heavy sigh.
Remembering how Krishna toughened him when he was weak,
Arjuna calmed himself, inhaled, and raised his head to speak.

"Lord Krishna has departed. We're alone now, Yudhiṣṭhir.
My strength in war, which stunned the gods, has also disappeared.
I must discuss Lord Krishna first, for I feel such remorse,
the universe seems empty and as lifeless as a corpse.

When we and other princes sought the hand of Draupadī,
King Draupada, her father, made impossible decrees
to pierce a fish-shaped target's eye, as tiny as a dot.
But Krishna steered my arrow to exactly the right spot.

One time the gods of rain and fire fought over some vale.
Lord Krishna helped me stop the rain so fire could prevail.

The demon Maya feared the flames, but Krishna heard his call,
and grateful Maya built for us our grand assembly hall.

One time the wretch Jarāsandha had kidnapped many kings,
so Krishna brought our Bhīma to confront him in the ring.
When Bhīma struggled, Krishna deftly showed him what to do,
and Bhīma grabbed his leg and ripped the demon's frame in two.

The sons of Dhṛtarāṣṭra snatched the hair of Draupadī,
and started to disrobe her as we stood there helplessly.
Lord Krishna stopped those scoundrels, and He later took their lives,
and left a widow's loosened hair upon their grieving wives.

And one time in the forest, when our food was at an end,
the volatile Durvāsā came for lunch with many friends.
Lord Krishna smiled and ate one scrap, and then, without delay,
Durvāsā and his entourage felt full and went away.

Lord Krishna once conveyed me to the heavenly abode
where Śiva kindly gave to me his own Gāṇḍīva bow.
With Krishna at my side I helped the gods to win a war,
but Krishna is now gone, and I am weaker than before.

What else but Krishna's friendship made us able to withstand
the threats imposed by Dhṛtarāṣṭra's sons upon our clan?
Though Bhīṣma and so many other heroes took their side,
we simply stayed with Krishna, and now all of them have died.

When all those Kuru heroes turned their deadly swords on me,
Lord Krishna's grace protected me from any injury.
Like me, the young Prahlād survived the tortures he went through
till Krishna as Nṛsiṁha killed Hiranyakaśipu.

I watered all my horses in that Kurukṣetra war
where enemies abounded, and yet I was just ignored.
Lord Krishna made this happen, yet I foolishly retained
the Lord of all the universe to hold my horses' reins.

Oh Yudhiṣṭhir, I see His face, His warm, enchanting smile.
I hear His voice addressing me in sweet, informal style:
'O Son of Kuntī, my dear friend, great hero of the realm....'
as I remember Krishna now, my heart is overwhelmed.

Lord Krishna dined, relaxed and spoke with me, His friend, each day.
As I felt quite familiar, I would tease the Lord and say,
'Oh, You are very truthful,' as He made some clever ploy.
He'd smile at me exactly as a father greets his boy."

AN UNPRECEDENTED DEFEAT (41-49)

The trembling Arjuna raised his eyes to Yudhiṣṭhir
and said, "Disaster struck us as we made our way back here.
Lord Krishna's wives were helpless, so I brought them here to stay.
And then a gang of thieves appeared and stole them all away!

I was the "great Arjuna," so-called hero of such fame.
My bow and arrows, chariot and horses were the same.
Without Lord Krishna, I became as useless, in a flash,
as seeds cast over barren land or ghee poured over ash.

The fate of all our friends in Dvārakā is even worse.
They had a drunken fight among themselves, for they were cursed.
Their battle was so vicious, it seemed no one would survive.
Now all of them are dead, I think, except for four or five.

I know all these disasters are, in fact, Lord Krishna's will.
Though sometimes people help each other, sometimes people kill.
Lord Krishna, seeing no one who could match His army's worth
has let them kill each other, thus unburdening the Earth.

When I gave up my duty in the Kurukṣetra war,
Lord Krishna kindly counseled me until I felt restored.
The sweet and holy lessons that I heard the Lord impart
still fascinate my shattered mind and ease my burning heart."

Recalling Krishna's sacred words with loving dedication,
Arjuna stopped abruptly and slipped into meditation.
By contemplating deeply what Lord Krishna did and said,
Arjuna seemed to calm the storm that raged within his head.

Arjuna's pain appeared to be unbearably intense
'til Krishna's words returned to him, restoring common sense.
By consciousness of Krishna, he transcended any doubt.
He saw the wheel of birth and death and readied to get out.

He saw that Krishna comes and goes by choice and not by force,
unlike we souls who struggle as our karma runs its course.
He merged his thoughts in Krishna, who can magically take birth
to stop demonic multitudes from plundering the earth.

Arjuna's mother Kuntī listened as her son described
Lord Krishna's disappearance and the Yadu clan's demise.
Deciding she could still serve Krishna many different ways,
Queen Kuntī vowed to do just that throughout her final days.

YUDHIṢṬHIR GIVES UP THE THRONE (50-62)

To Yudhiṣṭhir, the shocking news was worse than he had feared,
but he had long prepared to act when Krishna disappeared.
That very instant he resolved to leave his worldly throne
and follow Krishna back to His eternal, blissful home.

The Kali-age set in the day that Krishna disappeared,
engulfing earth with hatred, lies and poisoned atmosphere.
Unlike those modern leaders who hang on until they rot,
King Yudhiṣṭhir renounced his throne without a further thought.

For Yudhiṣṭhir had tutored Viṣṇurāta like a son
to carry on the monarchy, and now that time had come.
As Viṣṇurāta scaled the throne, the citizens were pleased,
for he was fit to govern the great kingdom perfectly.

Then Yudhiṣṭhir placed Vajra, Krishna's grandson, in command
of Mathurā, the district famed as Krishna's sacred land.
Completing years of duty to his subjects, friends and wife,
now Yudhiṣṭhir held rituals to give up family life.

Relinquishing his splendid jewels, silks and royal belt,
and feeling more disinterested than he had ever felt,
the former king surrendered his whole body unto death
and blended, with the greater air, his body's living breath.

Then Yudhiṣṭhir concluded, as a soul, he had acquired
his earth-and-water body as the fruit of his desires.
Returning all the elements he'd borrowed for this spree,
he merged his life in spirit and behaved accordingly.

He dressed in ragged garments and untied his tidy hair,
and showed upon his face no more than silent, vacant stares.
Without consulting anyone, he started walking north,
and only thought of Krishna as he aimlessly went forth.

Observing what the king had done to greet the Kali age,
his younger brothers chose to do the same. They all could gauge
that irreligious Kali would extract a heavy toll,
infecting everybody with unworthy, evil goals.

The saintly sons of Pāṇḍu had encountered many trials.
They always followed scripture and did everything worthwhile.
That day they took the final step that makes a life complete
and fixed their minds entirely on Krishna's lotus feet.

Thus purified, the sons of Pāṇḍu kept themselves absorbed
in flawless meditation on their sweet, beloved Lord.
Lord Krishna gave all five a gift not usually attained:
admission, in their bodies, to His personal domain.

And meanwhile, wise Vidura, on a distant pilgrimage,
had also left his body in the manner of a sage.
Although he also fixed his mind on Krishna as he died,
Vidura went to be a god and not to Krishna's side.

Bereft of loving husbands, Draupadī was left alone,
but she was fully trained to think of Krishna on her own.
So when the time arrived for her to leave this mortal plane,
by Krishna's grace she reached that place her husbands had attained.

The pastime of the Pāṇḍavas departing from this world
compares with Krishna's pastimes, for it's absolutely pure.
A faithful soul who listens to it well from start to end
arouses pure devotion to Lord Krishna deep within.

STRATEGY #9: THINK OF KRISHNA

Thinking of Krishna is a simple yet surprisingly powerful strategy for success in life. The fortunate Arjuna heard the *Bhagavad-gītā* directly from Krishna just before the Battle of Kuruksetra. Following Krishna's instruction to think of Him while fighting, Arjuna and his brothers won the great war. Now, with Krishna's departure, the Pandavas along with Draupadī and Kuntī are overwhelmed with grief. It is Krishna's same instruction—to always think of Him—that gives them the strength to rise above it all and carry on.

Thinking of Krishna in bhakti-yoga forges a strong connection that enables the bhakta to feel Krishna's presence in all circumstances. To remember Krishna, the beautiful, loving, supreme controller, immediately drives away anxiety and regret. When troubles come, a bhakta can shift his or her mood from despair to hope just by thinking of Krishna.

Because he loved Krishna so much, in his intense pain Arjuna managed to think of Him . However, when we're just getting to know Krishna and are still attached to material things, it can be difficult to remember Krishna. Though the soul is naturally attracted to Krishna, the materialistic atmosphere of today's world covers the soul's pure consciousness as clouds cover the sun.

The materially covered soul is like a rusty nail. Iron nails are naturally drawn to a magnet, but when rust covers a nail there will be no attraction. As soon as the rust is removed, the cleansed iron regains its natural magnetic attraction. In the same way, as soon as our consciousness is purified, our minds will naturally be drawn to Krishna, whose very name means, "The All-attractive One."

To restore our pure spiritual consciousness we need to hear pure spiritual sound. The most powerful spiritual sounds are the names of the Supreme. Such sounds are called mantras, a Sanskrit word meaning a sound that frees (tra) the mind (man). Any name of the Supreme can be recited as a mantra with great benefit. The Vedic literature recommends the Hare Krishna mantra—Hare Krishna, Hare Krishna, Krishna Krishna, Hare Hare, Hare Rāma, Hare Rāma, Rāma Rāma, Hare Hare—as most direct and beneficial. This mantra is a petition to the Supreme to allow us to serve. Attentively hearing the sound vibration created by repeating this mantra quickly revives our pure spiritual consciousness.

Of course, to think about someone we need to know something about them. Otherwise what are we going to think about? We get to know someone by listening to what they say, by hearing about what they do, or by finding out what others have to say about them. Fortunately, we have easy access to all these sources of information about Krishna.

For example, we can know what Krishna said by reading the *Bhagavad-gītā*. A Sanskrit phrase meaning, "The song of the Supreme," *Bhagavad-gītā* brims with instructions, encouragement and words of wisdom. The *Bhāgavat Purāṇa* tells us of Krishna's activities, His qualities, and even what He looks like. All this information is given by Krishna Himself or by spiritually advanced bhaktas who have personally seen and interacted with Krishna. In addition to chanting we can also read these great literatures and become more familiar with the Supreme Personality, Krishna.

Once we are a bit practiced in hearing and chanting about Krishna, we can deepen our awareness of ourselves and our place in this world by meditating on these basic philosophical points:

- *I am not this body;*
- *Everything happens under Krishna's control;*
- *This world is not meant for my enjoyment.*

Later, as we gain realization of Krishna's hand in our lives, we can reflect in a more personal way, reminding ourselves that:

- *Krishna is my friend;*
- *Krishna is teaching me something;*
- *Krishna is kindly helping me turn to Him to permanently end these constant ups and downs.*

When things are going well we may fail to thank Krishna. For that reason, troubles can be a blessing, for, like Arjuna, troubles force us to remember Krishna. Those who practice bhakti yoga learn to remember Krishna in all circumstances and thus remain peaceful and calm.

The abovementioned bhakti-yoga practices—chanting the Hare Krishna mantra, studying the *Bhagavad-gītā* and *Bhāgavat Purāṇa*, and making a conscious mental effort to remember Krishna in our daily lives—are easy to do. They become even easier when we do them in the company of other bhaktas.

It's not that we are "down here," and Krishna is far away "up there." Krishna can be as close to us as we want Him to be. These simple practices quickly awaken our dormant love for Krishna. Then, not only will we be thinking more of Krishna, but Krishna will be thinking more of us.

TEN

DHARMA

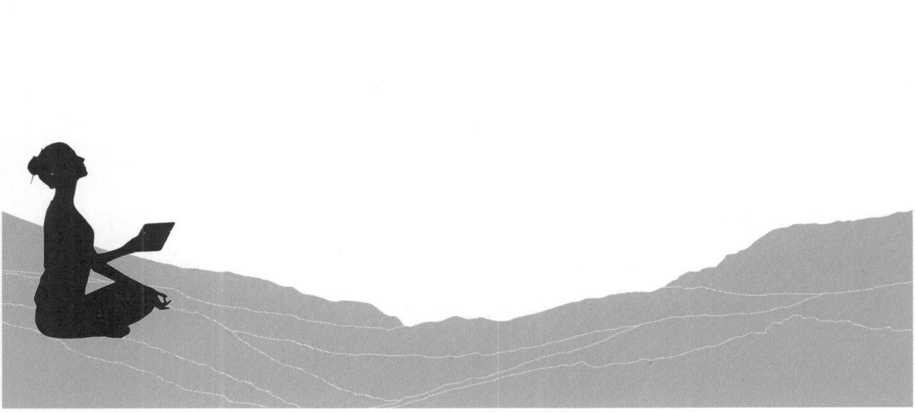

AN EXCEPTIONAL CRIME (1-12)

When Viṣṇurāta took the throne, he firmly set his mind
to follow the example of King Pāṇḍu's royal line.
Directed by the saintly priests, this great, devoted soul
presided well and wisely as the sages had foretold.

King Viṣṇurāta married and had four sons with his wife.
His guru Kṛpā helped him with his spiritual life.
On Gaṅgā's banks the king performed such splendid sacrifice
that gods revealed their presence to the common person's eyes.

One day, when Viṣṇurāta toured to scrutinize his lands,
he saw a rogue dressed as a king with bludgeon in his hand.
This Kali-age personified was beating bull and cow.
King Viṣṇurāta punished him, for this was not allowed.

As Sūta told these stories in consecutive narration,
the sages sat in perfect silence, rapt in concentration.
The news of beaten cows, however, stirred the silent crowd,
so Śaunaka, their spokesman, promptly stood and said aloud,

"Dear Sūta, thank you very much for speaking in this way.
The god of death, Lord Yamarāj, has even come today
to hear these talks of Krishna, for he understands their worth;
the listener will also die, but then has no more birth.

Your Krishna-talk is honey sweet and endlessly sublime.
What is the use of hearing news that simply wastes one's time?
A fool cares not for Krishna-talk and spends his time instead
all day pursuing money and all night enjoying bed.

We want to know why Viṣṇurāta did not kill the man
who bludgeoned helpless cows and bulls. It's hard to understand.
Was not the scoundrel killed at once for such a dreadful sin?
As this relates to Krishna, Sūta, kindly speak again."

So Sūta said, As Viṣṇurāta studied, he could tell
that Kali-age was infiltrating, raising social hell.
Determined to correct the faults and set his kingdom right,
he left to find and challenge Kali to a proper fight.

The King went out in person to inspire his mighty forces,
his lion-flagged, swift chariot pulled on by four black horses.
His fearless soldiers marched or rode on elephants with jewels
and subjugated distant lands to Viṣṇurāta's rule.

Beholding this unrivalled army, monarchs joined their palms
and loudly praised the Pāṇḍavas while paying royal alms.
When kings declared, "Lord Krishna saved you, even in the womb!"
King Viṣṇurāta's eyes lit up and he allotted boons.

King Viṣṇurāta heard how Krishna very humbly served
and helped the sons of Pāndu gain the kingdom they deserved.
He drove Arjuna's chariot and guided Bhīma's club.
These pastimes of Lord Krishna filled the young king's heart with love.

King Viṣṇurāta passed his days just hearing of the glories
of Krishna and the Pāṇḍavas in celebrated stories.
While on this journey, Viṣṇurāta too made history,
so listen well, dear sages, and you'll learn of this from me.

DHARMA AND MOTHER EARTH CONSOLE EACH OTHER (13-31)

One day a bull named Dharma (who was truth personified)
approached a cow (the Earth herself) who piteously cried.
She looked just like a mother with a child now lost or dead.
Concerned with her condition, Dharma limped to her and said,

"Dear Madam, you were always healthy, grazing on this hill.
How has this wave of sorrow caught you? Are you feeling ill?
Has something awful frightened you, discoloring your face?
Has your beloved left you for a distant, dangerous place?

I only have a single leg; I've lost the other three.
Have you become unhappy at the very sight of me?
As citizens have spurned the gods and lost their drink and food,
do they now want to eat your flesh? Has mankind grown that crude?

Do fathers leave their wives and kids for any selfish whim?
Do so-called learned priests become the slaves of many sins,
while disrespectful rulers keep them happy on the dole?
Has all this degradation shred the fabric of your soul?

The people of this Kali-age behave themselves like beasts
who dine on flesh, expose themselves, and care not in the least.
The great administrators of this brute society
won't even lift a finger to restore propriety.

Dear Mother Earth, Lord Krishna came to mitigate the pain
inflicted by atrocious kings whose greed drives them insane.
To simply think of Krishna's deeds assures our liberation.
Do you now weep and suffer from Lord Krishna's separation?

When Krishna walked your surface, all the gods in heaven sighed
and felt intensely jealous of your fortune and your pride.
Now time, alas, has changed your fate, and you appear so weak
I wonder if you even have the energy to speak."

"I'll try my best to answer," said the Earth personified.
She gathered her composure as she brushed her tears aside.
"It pains me so to see you crippled, dear and noble friend.
You used to have four solid legs on which I could depend.

Your leg known as austerity no longer bears your weight.
Your leg known as compassion has been broken out of hate.
Your leg of sanitation seems to be completely gone,
and truthfulness alone remains, just barely hanging on.

I suffer at the sight of you, but even more I cry
for Krishna has departed for the spiritual sky.
With Krishna gone, the earth becomes a toy for Kali-age.
The might of Kali's power has reduced me to this stage.

Lord Krishna is the reservoir of truth and cleanliness
and all these other attributes a person may possess:
Control of raging anger and the trait of being kind;
Confidence, straightforwardness, and steadiness of mind;

Mastery of the senses, and responsibility;
Fairness, even mindedness and equanimity;
Education; faithfulness; divine austerity;
Influential leadership; heartfelt chivalry;

Triumph over obstacles; adherence to one's duty;
Self-reliance; aptitude; extraordinary beauty;

Thoughtfulness; resourcefulness; a life of harmony;
Willpower; intelligence; respect and courtesy;
Firmness; perfect knowledge; the resources to enjoy;
Joyfulness itself; impressive power, well deployed;
Worthiness of being worshipped; absence of false pride;
Steadiness and fame; in Krishna, all these traits reside.

Though Krishna's very presence kept the Kali-age in check,
now everybody suffers Kali's horrible effects.
So, I despair for you and me, the gods and saintly souls,
and all the decent people in varnashram social roles.

Impressing marks of thunderbolts and flags and lotus flowers,
Lord Krishna's footprints graced my soil, investing me with power.
The goddess Lakṣmī, Queen of wealth, whom all the gods entreat,
departs her lotus-filled abode for Krishna's lotus feet.

I once was overburdened due to atheistic kings,
'till Krishna smashed their armies and relieved my suffering.
My dear religious Dharma, demons brought you misery,
'till Krishna graced the human race and Yadu dynasty.

If once one sees Lord Krishna, can one bear to be apart?
His wives protested when he left, but Krishna charmed their hearts.
Though Krishna sometimes left His wives, His feet could not leave me,
and where he walked my grass stood up like hairs in ecstasy."

As Mother Earth and Dharma thus conversed as bull and cow
and comforted themselves as far as circumstance allowed,
the mighty Viṣṇurāta and his entourage arrived
and rested on the nearby Sarasvatī riverside.

KALI CHASTISED (32-40)

King Viṣṇurāta looked and saw a shocking spectacle,
a low-class man in royal garments bludgeoning a bull.
The pure-white bull, too frightened to negotiate or beg,
just trembled and passed urine on his one remaining leg.

Beside the bull, a lovely cow, the emblem of all good,
withdrew in terror as the scoundrel beat her where she stood.
Distressed and weak, with teary eyes and no calf at her teat,
she hankered just to find a grassy field where she could eat.

King Viṣṇurāta watched this blatant sin with shock and wonder.
With bow in hand, he screamed out, in a voice as loud as thunder,
"Immoral rogue, how dare you strike this helpless bull and cow?
Though dressed up as a monarch, your behavior is most foul!

With Krishna and Arjuna gone, have you become so bold
to beat a harmless cow as if my lands were unpatrolled?
You think you will be safe in this remote, secluded place?
You demon, I'll destroy you and protect the human race."

The King then asked the wounded bull, "Who are you, my dear friend?
You seem to be a god who has elected to descend.
At no time in the history of our ancient royal line
has anybody suffered such an irreligious crime.

Dear bull, you needn't worry. You are well protected now.
And you may also dry your tears, O gentle mother cow.
As long as I am living, I shall thoroughly subdue
debauchees like this rascal who has been attacking you.

When cows are hurt, the king shall forfeit everything of worth,
his life, his reputation and auspicious future births.
Religious kings protect the weak from those who wish them ill.
This wretched, violent man must be immediately killed!

The Pāṇḍu kings rebuke those who ignore the scripture's laws,
unless there's an emergency or reasonable cause.
The gods themselves shall feel my strength and suffer from my wrath
should they abuse my subjects and pursue an evil path.

The scriptures guide my kingdom, and my subjects are secure.
How dare this cruel person break the legs of one so pure?
Offenseless bull, who is this man who mutilates your frame
and undermines the glories of our royal family name?"

KALI SPARED (41-62)

The bull looked very thankful and respectfully replied,
"Your words befit the Pāṇḍu line, which you exemplify.
Your forefathers created such an ideal atmosphere
that God Himself, Lord Krishna, came to serve King Yudhiṣṭhir.

Dear King, it is quite hard to say by whom we are abused.
Philosophers debate this point, but they too seem confused.
Some say we cause our own distress when we commit a sin,
while others say that higher powers rule the lives of men.

And some declare that nature causes random joy and grief,
while others claim that action rules, rejecting all belief.
And some conclude that suffering can never be explained.
In light of all these points of view, what do you ascertain?"

King Viṣṇurāta heard all this with pleasure and surprise
for he did not expect a philosophical reply.
"My dear religious bull," he said, "you tactfully refuse
to blame your foe and reap the fate of he whom you accuse.

Personified Religion, in your awe-inspiring way
you do not fault this man who has abused you here today.
And yet your troubles aren't explained by such philosophy,
for God Himself alone controls a person's destiny.

The Kali-age's influence has broken your three limbs.
The first of them, austerity, succumbed to prideful whims.
Another leg, compassion, fell to gross intoxication;
Your other leg of cleanliness was lost to fornication.

Upheld by one remaining leg, you somehow hobble on.
That final leg is truthfulness. It too is almost gone,
for Kali-age proliferates in lying and deceit.
When truth collapses, Kali-age's triumph is complete.

Lord Krishna, with assistance from devoted, pious souls,
had recently exalted Earth and eased her heavy load.
Alone now as a cow, she worries, teardrops in her eyes,
while low-class men exploit her any way they can devise."

King Viṣṇurāta calmed the bull and cow with pleasing words.
Considering their agony and all they had endured,
that fearsome warrior turned and gazed on Kali-age's head,
and drew his sword to pierce him and make sure the rogue was dead.

The Kali-age personified, distributor of strife,
could see the king was furious and set to take his life.

The Kali-age could not fight back as kings do, so instead,
he dropped his phony royal dress and bowed his trembling head.

On seeing Kali supplicate and put no battle forward,
King Viṣṇurāta gently smiled and sheathed his gleaming sword.
King Viṣṇurāta never killed surrendered souls, you see.
That's why his great compassion is acclaimed in history.

King Viṣṇurāta said, "Arjuna always spared the man
who knelt in supplication and presented folded hands.
So you may live, but you must leave my kingdom right away,
for every kind of sin would thrive were I to let you stay.

No, you do not deserve to stay where goodness is the norm,
and sacrifice for Krishna is so expertly performed.
In our kingdom a sacrifice for god or man or king
is offered just for Krishna, Lord Supreme of everything."

Now Kali trembled nervously as Viṣṇurāta spoke,
and fearfully addressed the King, his voice barely a croak:

"You rule the very earth, O King, so anywhere I go
I know you will await me with your arrows and your bow.
You've seen my evil nature and you know what to expect;
just spare my life, and I shall stay wherever you direct."

King Viṣṇurāta studied Kali, thought a bit and said,
"I grant you life where couples join illicitly in bed.
And you may also live where men drink liquor in the street,
make wagers and kill animals to dine upon their meat."

Now Kali was quite clever and he very clearly knew
that no such place existed under Viṣṇurāta's rule.
He said, "Thank you, my King. If my request is not too bold,
please also let me live wherever men are hoarding gold."

When greedy people choose to issue paper backed by gold
they print more notes and currency than wealth they really hold.
And yet, King Viṣṇurāta took in Kali on that basis,
and told him he could live in any one of those five places.

The gathering of gold creates a tainted atmosphere
where liquor, meat, illicit sex and gambling appear.
A leader, priest, renunciate and any moral soul
should carefully avoid these sins in blissful self-control.

King Viṣṇurāta sheltered Kali in a clever way,
for he began to gather all his kingdom's gold that day.
He used the funds to put together Dharma's broken limbs,
and brought the Earth contentment so she flourished once again.

For how can there be honesty when gambling is allowed,
and how can there be mercy among those who slaughter cows?
Can prostitutes be clean or can a drunk be self-controlled?
King Viṣṇurāta stopped all this by proper use of gold.

Enlightened sages, you are here by Viṣṇurāta's grace
for he restored religion and put Kali in his place.
When kings and priests are pure, the common man is satisfied,
but where there is corruption, Kali will not be denied.

STRATEGY #10: FORGIVE

In this section, King Viṣṇurāta discovers the current Kali-age personified cruelly beating Dharma the bull, who is tottering on one as yet unbroken leg. 'Dharma' refers to morality and duty, and Viṣṇurāta catches Kali as he is about to kill Dharma. Kali's identity is quite clear since he's standing next to his victim, weapon in hand. Yet when Viṣṇurāta asks Dharma who has caused his suffering, Dharma does not blame his attacker. Instead he philosophizes and asks the king's opinion. Was it his karma coming back to him? Was it the astrological influence of the planets? Was it due to his own lack of mental equilibrium? Or was it the will of the Supreme?

By overlooking the immediate cause of his pain and considering possible remote causes, including divine will, Dharma exhibits his saintliness and makes it much easier to exercise forgiveness. When someone wrongs us, forgiving them can be extremely difficult. Our minds may insist that forgiving the wrongdoer would allow them to hurt us again. However, if we fail to forgive one who has hurt us, we do more harm to ourselves than to our antagonist.

Failing to forgive means we hold a grudge against those who hurt us. This grudge is like a sore spot on our hearts that pains us throughout our lives. If we never forgive that person, we carry that grudge to our grave. The *Bhagavad-gītā* explains that whatever we remember at death determines our next birth. Thus maintaining unresolved anger with a person who wronged us means we may have to be around them for yet another lifetime!

Human beings share with animals four powerful urges: eating, sleeping, mating and defending. Of these four impulses, the urge to defend oneself is said to be the strongest. When someone hurts us, we want to retaliate, to lash out. A yogī can overcome this instinct by remembering that forgiving those who hurt us is for our benefit, not theirs.

Even if we understand this approach in our mind, it can be hard to feel forgiveness in our heart. Here are some additional tips:

- Try to see things from the other person's point of view by thinking, "Perhaps if I were in this person's circumstances, I would have done the same thing."
- Cut your losses by thinking, "What I really want is to never associate with this hurtful person again. Therefore, let me forgive and forget so I can move on as quickly as possible and focus on my relationships with people whom I love and who love me."
- As far as possible, without exposing yourself to any further association with the wrongdoer, think of them in a positive way, as a fellow human being, however flawed. This brings more peace of mind than hating the antagonist.
- See your antagonist as an agent of your own karma. After all, if we had not decided to leave Krishna in the first place and ended up in this world, we would not have suffered this abuse. Through this person, Krishna is kindly reminding us of our original mistake and convincing us to finish this life gracefully and have nothing more to do with this world.

In this passage, both Dharma and Viṣhnurāta show forgiveness. The sight of Kali hurting a bull and a cow at first shocked Viṣhnurāta so much that he prepared to execute Kali on the spot. However, when Kali surrendered in fear, the king put down his sword and forgave Kali while at the same time banishing him to an unsettled life. This teaches us a good lesson: forgiveness does not mean freeing the offender from punishment. A criminal must be justly prosecuted, both to rectify the criminal and protect others.

Usually we can't impose punishment on a wrongdoer, so forgiveness makes even more sense. If I drink poison, it will not hurt my antagonist. If I let go of negative feelings of animosity or vengeance, I will bathe my heart in the warm nectar of forgiveness and go on peacefully with my life. And a life well-lived is the best revenge.

Forgiving and forgetting is far better than fighting. As George Bernard Shaw said, "I learned long ago, never wrestle with a pig. You get dirty and the pig likes it."

ELEVEN

VIṢṆURĀTA

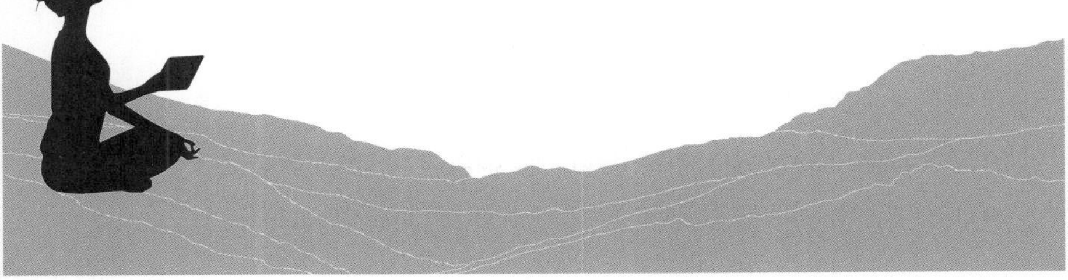

POTENT DISCUSSIONS OF KRISHNA (1-13)

I wish to praise King Viṣṇurāta; then we can resume.
When Droṇa's son attacked, Lord Krishna saved him in the womb.
He always thought of Krishna, so when it became quite clear
a deadly snake would kill him, Viṣṇurāta felt no fear.

King Viṣṇurāta left his throne and sat with Śukadev
to hear about Lord Krishna for his seven final days.
Those people who can hear and think of Krishna always thrive,
and risk no misconceptions when the time of death arrives.

The Kali-age is powerful and eager to begin
to saturate society with every type of sin.
Though Kali-age personified appeared the very day
Lord Krishna left our planet, Viṣṇurāta blocked his way.

While holding Kali back, King Viṣṇurāta felt no rage,
for he knew Krishna made concessions for this fallen age.
In other ages, sin accrues by leaving thoughts unchecked;
in Kali, one must act on sin to reap the sin's effect.

King Viṣṇurāta knew that Kali frightens foolish souls,
but could not touch the people who retain their self-control.
The King thus sheltered people as a tiger shields her cubs,
by teaching them to serve Lord Krishna's lotus feet with love.

Dear sages, as you asked me, I have told you everything
pertaining to Lord Krishna and the pious Pāṇḍu king.
Submissive souls like you who hear the topics of the Lord
attain the highest excellence a human life affords.

The sages glanced among themselves then answered as if one:
“Dear Sūta, your descriptions are delightfully well-done.
To hear you speak of Krishna has infused our hearts with hope,
while sacrificial fires only blacken us with smoke.

A moment of your presence is worth more, we all believe,
than money, fame, or anything a person might achieve,
for you have brought us Krishna, whom the gods cannot describe.
We’d love to hear you speak for the remainder of our lives.

Please carry on, dear Sūta, for we know that there is more
concerning Viṣṇurāta and the pastimes of the Lord.
Your talk surpasses anything we’ve ever come across.
What else did you find out from the enlightened son of Vyās?”

Said Sūta, All your praise makes me embarrassed, I confess,
for I was born in lower caste than those whom I address.
Because I served and heard from more enlightened devotees,
the potency of Krishna-talk has lifted even me.

Lord Krishna has no master, but He’s effortlessly claimed
by one who always glorifies and sings His holy name.
The gods chase after Lakṣmī, seeking wealth for many births,
yet she serves only Krishna, who seeks no reward from her.

So who else could be God but Krishna? Who else can compete?
The Gaṇgā’s waters purify because they touch His feet.
A soul attached to Krishna can leave any situation
and find the peace and happiness of full renunciation.

So let us speak of Krishna as completely as we can,
as birds traverse the sky with all the strength at their command.

VIṢṆURĀTA CURSED (14-27)

Once Viṣṇurāta took his bow and arrow to the woods
for sharpening his martial skills, as royal hunters could.
As Viṣṇurāta chased his prey, his thirst began to rage.
Just then he found the cottage of a meditating sage.

His beard and matted hair askew, the sage was deep in trance,
unmindful of his royal guest and outer circumstance.
With burning throat too dry for him to pause and clearly think,
King Viṣṇurāta blurted, "Have you water here to drink?"

You know our culture very well, so I need not repeat
that hosts must always offer greetings, water and a seat.
The sage, however, stayed in trance, completely unaware
a noble but neglected guest grew angry standing there.

Though usually quite patient, on this day, by Krishna's will,
King Viṣṇurāta took offense and wished the brahman ill.
Deciding that the so-called trance was nothing but a fake,
he garlanded that brahman with a harmless, lifeless snake.

As Viṣṇurāta left that place he felt some slight remorse,
but he could not see how his deed would alter history's course.
At that time, in the woods nearby, the sage's childish son
was told by all his playmates what the angry king had done.

The sage's son (named Śṛṅgi) said, "Like noisy dogs or crows,
such kings insult the brahman class, who everybody knows
are meant to head society. This king has grown so proud,
he's like a dog who sneaks and eats some food he's not allowed.

Since Krishna's disappearance, all these kings have been a bother.
Just watch as I rebuke this man who mistreated my father!"
Now Śṛṅgi was quite powerful but much too young to tell
that what he would do next would suit the Kali-age so well.

His eyes red-hot with anger, Śṛṅgi muttered sacred verse,
and called to all his playmates, "Now, behold a brahman's curse!
In seven days, this king will die of deadly snake-bird bite.
If one insults a brahman, such a death will serve him right."

The boy then marched to see his father, full of childish pride.
With every step, he felt more guilt, and suddenly, he cried.
The sound disturbed the sage's trance, and as he came awake,
he saw his sobbing son and felt the cold and sagging snake.

He brushed the snake aside and asked, "My son, why do you cry?"
The boy explained the snake and how he cursed the King to die.
The sage cried out, "Alas! My son, you lost your common sense
and cursed a pious king for a most trivial offense.

My son, you're inexperienced. You do not understand.
A godly king protects us all. He's not some common man.
The king embodies God Himself! Without his guiding hand,
the thieves will plunder all of us like unprotected lambs.

Possessions stolen, women raped, and people hurt or dead—
if we have killed the king, these sins fall squarely on our head.
The people will grow godless in their sensual escape.
Ignoring Vedic social rules, they'll live like dogs and apes.

The good King Viṣṇurāta is a first-class devotee.
His godliness makes him a saint among the royalty.

When such a king is hot and tired, suffering from thirst,
he should be given water, but instead, he has been cursed.

Dear Krishna, all-pervading Lord, excuse my foolish son!
His actions are just opposite of what he should have done.
A brahman helps the king do well for everybody's sake,
but Śṛṅgi cursed the monarch for a very slight mistake.

This king could free himself and take revenge, were he inclined,
but devotees of Krishna are, by nature, very kind.
So even when dishonored or neglected or repressed,
a king like Viṣṇurāta doesn't feel himself distressed."

VIṢHNURĀTA RENOUNCES HIS LIFE (28-44)

As Viṣṇurāta grew more guilty for his thoughtless deed,
he thought aloud, "I know my sin has placed a wicked seed
of pain and karma sure to bloom and devastate my life.
Lord Krishna, let me suffer, but please spare my sons and wife.

A common man's transgression may be sometimes disavowed,
but Kings must always worship Krishna, brahman priests and cows.
So, let my strength and riches burn before this brahman's wrath
and I shall take another birth and walk a better path."

Reflecting thus, the thoughtful Viṣṇurāta was apprised
about the curse of Śṛṅgi and his forthcoming demise.
"This news about my death is very welcome," thought the king.
"It makes me apathetic to all ordinary things."

At once renouncing royal crown, majestic robes and throne,
the saintly Viṣṇurāta went to Gaṅgā's banks alone.
Her waters mixed with Krishna-dust and sacred tulsi leaves,
the Gaṅgā is auspicious for those soon to be bereaved.

The King felt blessed to know he had but seven days to live,
for that is far more notice than death usually gives.
Rejecting other practices like garbage in the street,
he fixed his mind entirely on Krishna's lotus feet.

The worthy heir of Pāṇḍu's throne resolved to sit and fast
and only think of Krishna's feet until he breathed his last.
Renouncing all attachments to his kingdom, land and cows,
the king forsook his ministers and took a sage's vows.

As news of Viṣṇurāta's vows pervaded earth and space,
great sages, saints, and their disciples hurried to that place.
The glorious saint Nārada, with vina, quickly came,
along with famous gurus far too numerous to name.

As many great souls came together, gathering around,
the former monarch bowed to each, his forehead to the ground.
Preparing to face death without the weight of past offense,
a wise man gives respect to others out of common sense.

The many sages sat at ease on Gaṅgā's sacred sands
as Viṣṇurāta stood and spoke to them with folded hands:
"Among all kings I feel most blessed because you're here today,
for sages often shun us kings and keep themselves away.

The greatest person, Krishna, kindly took me by surprise
by coming as a brahman's curse and bringing my demise.

I feel that I am so attached to mundane life and wealth
that I'll become detached by nothing less than death itself.

Oh learned sages, Mother Gaṅgā, hear my simple goal:
I pray that you accept me as a most surrendered soul.
Now kindly chant Lord Krishna's glories as I meet my fate
from snake-bird bite or anything the brahman's curse creates.

I prostrate at your feet, great souls, and pray that, should I take
another birth within this world, I'll live for Krishna's sake.
And in that life, I also pray, dear sages, if you please,
that I stay friends with everyone and live with devotees."

Then Viṣṇurāta sat himself. His worldly work was done,
for he had left the kingdom to his righteous elder son.
He sat on sacred kuśa grass and faced the northern sky,
and then and there, on Gaṅgā's bank, prepared himself to die.

Observing this, the gods above were greatly overcome.
They praised the King and showered flowers, beating sacred drums.
The kindly sages also praised the King's courageous choice,
and rose to state their satisfaction with a single voice:

"The helmets of a hundred kings adorn your royal throne,
yet we are not surprised to see you come here all alone.
The Pāṇḍavas knew life is meant for praising Krishna's name,
and as their true descendant, your conclusion is the same.

So we shall watch, King Viṣṇurāta, as you leave this plane
for Krishna's own abode, which lies beyond deceit and pain."
Acknowledging the sages words as sweet, sincere and true,
The king replied, "I thank you, sirs. May I inquire from you?

You've gathered here, so wise and good and graciously inclined.
In this life or the next, you simply want to serve mankind.
Please tell me of that duty with which all men must comply
and, more specifically, for one who's just about to die."

ŚUKADEVA ARRIVES (45-54)

Now, at that moment there appeared the mighty son of Vyās,
apparently meandering, yet not appearing lost.
He wore no clothes and seemed unfit for any social class.
A crowd of children stared at him and giggled as he passed.

His name was Śukadev, and he was sixteen, you recall,
when he left home for Krishna, brushing off his father's calls.
His youthful torso, legs and arms, and sweet, attractive face
were handsome, wide and beautiful, and very nicely placed.

His manly body sported arms of strong and lengthy type,
with navel set in abdomen of deeply muscled stripes.
His hair hung black and curly, and his lustrous body's hue
reflected that of Krishna, an enchanting blackish-blue.

The women were attracted, for his charming smile was sweet.
The sages also noticed him and rose up from their seats.
They knew of physiognomy, and since they could detect
that he was most enlightened, they extended their respects.

Then Viṣṇurāta bowed before this great, exalted guest,
while Śukadev exchanged his bows with Vyās and all the rest.

Surprised to see him taken to an elevated seat,
the children teasing Śukadev ran off in quick retreat.

Surrounded by the saints and sages gathered from afar,
young Śukadev shone forth just like the moon among the stars.
He sat and seemed prepared to fill his listeners' commands,
so Viṣṇurāta bowed again and said, with folded hands,

"Though I am just a lowly king, you've come to be my guest.
Your presence makes these sages and the Gaṅgā doubly blessed.
As atheists cannot remain where Krishna has appeared,
our sins depart when you arrive. You cleanse the atmosphere.

Lord Krishna must have sent you, for He loves our dynasty.
How could you otherwise have come across a man like me?
Please take me as your student. Now, for what should I aspire,
particularly at this time, when I shall soon expire?

How should I worship God before my body is destroyed?
What things should I remember, and what acts should I avoid?
You often stay just long enough for one to milk a cow.
Will you please stay to answer all my questions here and now?"

As questions flowed in pleasant speech from Abhimanyu's son,
the son of Vyās grew eager to respond to every one.
Resolving to assist the king and ready to comply,
the striking sage inhaled and smiled and started his reply.

[End of First Canto of the *Bhāgavat Purāṇa*]

STRATEGY #11: LET GO

The previous strategies for moving toward sainthood—being compassionate and forgiving, looking ahead realistically, setting spiritual priorities, striving for goodness and practicing bhakti-yoga under the guidance of a guru—all prepare us for this next one: letting go of material attachments. We come into this life with nothing more than our bodies, and as time goes by, we become attached to many extraneous things like our homes, our families, our friends, our possessions, our social positions, and so on. These things are all temporary. We will lose them all when we are forced to leave our present bodies.

Although we all know this fact, our minds remain attached to material things. Such attachment seems harmless unless we understand the soul. If we spiritual souls die with material attachments and desires, we will have to again take birth in the material world to fulfill them. As we have already discussed, any birth in the material world means suffering for the soul.

If we want to put a permanent end to all suffering we must make a conscious effort to move beyond material things and find pleasure in the spiritual.

In this section we have the perfect example of Viṣṇurāta, for if anyone had something to hold onto, he did. He was the undisputed emperor of a huge kingdom, with unimaginable power, fame, and wealth at his disposal. Nevertheless, when he heard that he would die in seven days, he didn't go on a binge nor did he protest. Instead he immediately renounced everything, took off his royal dress and handed his kingdom over to his son. He even gave up eating and sleeping. With nothing other than a simple cotton loincloth, he sat under a tree on the bank of the sacred Ganges, in the company of saints, to focus on spiritual topics in preparation for death.

One may wonder: if Viṣṇurāta had so much power, why didn't he fight his fate? Isn't that what we would do? After all, it was unfair, for his punishment was far more severe than his crime. Even the unqualified brahmana boy who cursed Viṣṇurāta came to regret rashly condemning such a good person and ideal king. If Viṣṇurāta had used his power to counteract the curse, all the citizens would have supported him.

But Viṣṇurāta was a saint, and saints see things differently. He understood that:

- There is a Supreme controller;
- this world is not our home; and
- one way or another, we'll be forced to leave our present body and situation.

Thus enlightened, Viṣṇurāta let go of everything and graciously embraced the fatal curse as the will of the Supreme.

One may also ask that if Viṣṇurāta knew he would die and had the power to stop it, was his acceptance of the deadly curse a form of suicide? Viṣṇurāta's situation was very different. Suicide is selfish, causing pain to loved ones and to the Supreme, who has given us life. In Viṣṇurāta's case, death had come to him, so he accepted it voluntarily. His choice enlightened others, so he accepted death as a service to the Supreme.

It could even be said that only after he accepted his death sentence did Viṣṇurāta really start to live. What Viṣṇurāta achieved in his last seven days could take many lifetimes for most of us. Finding a competent mentor, Śukadev, Viṣṇurāta asks a question which is relevant to us all: what should a person do when he or she is about to die?

Viṣṇurāta knew he had seven days. We may think we have seventy years, but we can't really say for sure whether we have even seven minutes. In any case there's no time to waste. The bhakta accepts responsibility for being a spirit stuck in a material body in the first place, and disentangles him or herself from material attachments. This detachment takes place automatically for one who practices hearing and chanting, as well as the other methods of bhakti-yoga.

The taste of bhakti is so powerful that it frees us from our most deeply rooted desires for pleasure, prestige and wealth. Such freedom does not excuse us from ordinary life and duties; it simply allows us to live as masters of desire, not its slaves, and to be 'in the world but not of it' while tending to our responsibilities.

By relaxing our embrace of this world and resolving all our issues beforehand, one feels more prepared for death, whenever it comes. Then, like Viṣṇurāta, we will have achieved equanimity and peace in bhakti-yoga, the ultimate success of human life.

TWELVE

ŚUKADEV

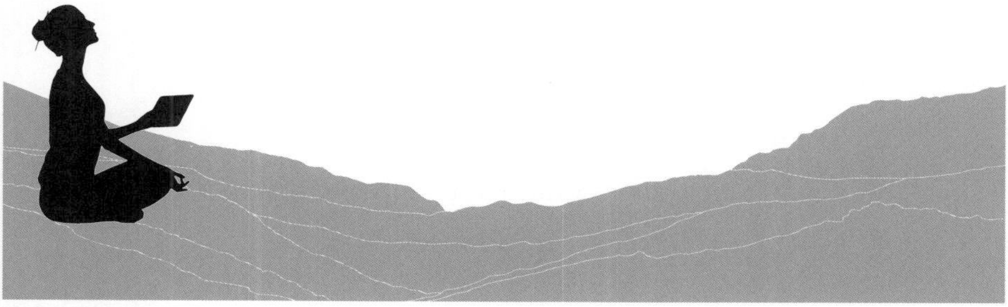

ŚUKADEV REPLIES (1-14)

"Dear King, your very question is magnificent and deep.
It sows a field of wisdom for the hands of all to reap.
The answers to your questions have already been endorsed
by learned transcendentalists, so let us start our course.

The ordinary person is materially engrossed
with endless themes for gossiping and countless fools to toast.
They chase down money in the day, have sex and sleep at night,
and hate their neighbors till they die, while thinking all is right.

Protected by the fragile troops of body, kids and spouse,
such people discount God and hope that death will skip their house.
Eternal souls though they may be, with many lifetimes past,
they foolishly construct another life that cannot last.

Enlightened souls, by contrast, rid themselves of worldly pains
by hearing and reciting Krishna's pastimes and His names.
The Supersoul who dwells within is no one else but He,
the mastermind of everything who ends one's misery.

So whether it's by scrutinizing spirit wrapped in skin,
or practicing some yoga till you grow austere and thin,
or filling your commitments to your country, kin and wife,
to think of Krishna as you die completes a perfect life.

Because of this, the topmost transcendentalists agree:
describing Krishna's glories is the greatest ecstasy.
When I was young and thought that God was something more abstract,
my father taught me *Bhāgavat* to help me get on track.

Although I fully understood that I was not my flesh,
Lord Krishna's pastimes caught my ear. They sounded sweet and fresh.
You've asked me, so I'll speak them now, as Vyās once did for me.
Your troubles will be finished if you hear attentively.

All those who have renounced the worldly pleasures of this life,
or those whose gross attractions for such pleasure are still rife,
or even those self-satisfied by wisdom they have gained,
can meet success by constantly repeating Krishna's name.

What use is it if you hang on until you're very old,
and waste a hundred years without awareness of the soul?
If you invest one moment asking who you really are
and start your search for truth, you will be better off by far.

The saintly King Khaṭvāṅga asked the gods when he would die.
'You'll die within a moment,' said the gods in swift reply.
The king was well prepared for death, and feeling no distress,
he promptly thought of Krishna and attained complete success.

My dear King Viṣṇurāta, you are blessed with much more time.
You've seven full remaining days to concentrate your mind.
Now you can meet approaching death without a trace of fear
by cutting ties to body, kin and all that you hold dear.

Yes, even leading people we might honor and admire
do not prepare themselves for death by changing their desire.
Desire will continue even when the body dies,
but if you just desire Krishna, death does not apply.

The first step is to understand that death comes unannounced,
so if you want to leave this world you must become renounced.

The self-controlled abandon all the comforts of the home
and sit down in a sacred place, content to utter 'oṁ'.

Though meditation starts this way, there's so much more, you see.
The mind must be subdued, dear king, but not repressively.
God's form is more attractive than a pure but formless sound,
so try to see the form of God pervading all around."

THE UNIVERSAL FORM (15-21)

"Dear Śukadev," *the king inquired*, "How does one absorb
the restless mind in Krishna as the all-pervading Lord?"

Said Śukadev, "The first step is to purify your mind
through yoga pose and breath control. Your thoughts will be refined.
Although Lord Krishna is much more, to start your meditation,
consider Him as He appears throughout the whole creation.

His universal body's feet are planets known as hell.
His head is formed of higher worlds where pious people dwell.
The cosmos is His eye socket; the sun globe is His eye;
His eyelids are the day and night that blink as time goes by.

The Lord of Death lives in His jaws, rebuking every sin.
His upper lip is modesty; desire is His chin.
Affection is His set of teeth, illusion is His smile,
and mountains are collections of His bones stacked up in piles.

The trees and shrubs comprise the universal body's hair.
The rivers are His veins. His breath consists of swirling air.

The ever-changing moon becomes His mind, so it is said,
and water-bearing clouds make up the hair upon His head.

His artistry appears in birds, like peacocks and the rest.
The singing gods exemplify His music at its best.
His face consists of priests, His arms the fearless warrior caste,
His thighs the wealthy merchants, and His feet the working class.

As ordinary persons manifest a thousand dreams,
Lord Krishna lives in everything, in countless ways and themes.
A person seeking liberation sees the Lord in all;
in truth, there is no other place a person's glance can fall.

WARNINGS AGAINST MATERIALISM (22-28)

In higher worlds the gods reside in pleasure-filled abodes.
Though hidden from our vision, they're described in Vedic codes.
The followers of Vedic texts show sterling qualities,
while foolish brutes will just accept what they can touch and see.

For those pursuing the Supreme, the chance sometimes appears
to join the gods in heaven for a thousand pleasant years.
A precious moment wasted seeking godly paradise
is history and cannot be bought back at any price.

Material desires lead to war and scarcity.
Why not accept a simple life without anxiety?
When you can sleep upon the floor with arms to prop your head,
what need is there for pillows and a splendid silken bed?

Are used clothes unavailable? Do trees not give their shade?
Do rivers now deny a man a drink on scorching days?
Will God ignore His servants who want nothing for themselves?
Then why should sages flatter those possessed of excess wealth?

While living in a world of names where nothing ever lasts,
where souls accept themselves as bodies built of sins amassed,
wherever you may find yourself, in any time or place,
just glorify Lord Krishna and recall His lovely face.

Approach the gods with some request or some complaint to lodge,
and you will always find a god who's willing to oblige.
But neither gods nor even Krishna's cosmic deity
can give you love of Krishna. That must come from devotees.

Perhaps you have transcended any taste for the mundane.
Perhaps you're feeling full of lust that's driving you insane.
Perhaps you simply want to merge in cosmic suicide.
In any case, just worship Krishna. You'll be purified."

ŚAUNAKA'S ECSTATIC REALIZATIONS (29-35)

These words of Śukadev, dear reader, to the dying king,
as Sūta had recounted to his eager gathering,
induced this speech by Śaunaka, the leader, you recall,
among the gathered sages. He stood up and said to all:

"These topics of Lord Krishna are entirely germane
to solving our dilemma. Please continue to explain.
As Śukadeva, the poet, and the pious king conversed,
there must have been more Krishna-talk in which we've been immersed.

The sun consumes our lifetimes as it rises and declines,
unless we choose to hear about Lord Krishna with our time.
Does any other action put our lives to better use?
Do trees not live, nor bellows breathe, nor creatures reproduce?

Those men who look and act like asses, camels, dogs and swine,
think other men who never hear of Krishna are just fine.
Without Krishna, one hears and speaks for someone else's sake
with lips and tongue like croaking frog and earholes like a snake.

A head packed full of godless facts is like a heavy crown:
on land it makes one popular; at sea, it makes one drown.
Those hands that never serve the Lord can only be compared
to those of a bejeweled corpse with lifeless, vacant stare.

The eyes that never look upon Lord Krishna's blissful form
are like the eyes with which a peacock's feathers are adorned.
The legs which fail to take one to a place where devotees
discuss Lord Krishna's glories are compared to trunks of trees.

A man who lacks the dust of saintly feet upon his head
or fails to smell a tulsi leaf may breathe, but he is dead.
A heart which fails to soften when the sound of Krishna's name
awakens dormant ecstasy is surely metal-framed.
Dear Sūta, with your pleasing words, continue to describe
what Śukadeva presented as the king prepared to die."

THE CREATION OF THE UNIVERSE (36-44)

Said Sūta, smiling, "Viṣṇurāta bowed his head and prayed,
'May I forever concentrate on Krishna, as you say.
Dear Śukadev, if it should suit the course of your narration,
please tell me how Lord Krishna manifests the whole creation.'"

Said Śukadeva, "These topics of the Lord alone can free
the speaker and the hearer from their past impurity.
By Krishna's power, Greeks and Turks and all those who reside
both in and out of India can all be purified.

The kingdom of the Lord exists within the lighted worlds
of Krishna's endless pastimes with the cowherd boys and girls.
A tiny, darkened corner of this boundless ecstasy
was set aside for such rebellious souls and you and me.

Lord Krishna never forces us to love Him. That would be
coercion, not affection that is given lovingly.
Lord Krishna simply wants our love, but if we turn our face
we opt to suffer death instead within that darkened place.

As darkness stands for ignorance, Lord Krishna manifests
Himself therein as Vishnu lying down to take some rest.
As Vishṇu sleeps in cosmic peace, His breath goes out and in,
and universes stream out of the pores upon His skin.

As He exhales, the countless universes manifest,
until He draws them in again as He fills up His chest.
The universe surrounding us is simply one of these:
one tiny, short-lived mustard seed within a ton of seeds.

Each coconut-like universe, with matter-layered hull,
and causal water ocean waves, with which it is half-full,
becomes home to another Vishṇu, smaller, but complete,
reclining on a serpent-raft while Lakṣmī rubs His feet.

The navel of this Vishṇu then expels a lotus sprout,
and in that dark and empty sky a lotus bud comes out.
Its petals peel, revealing Lord Brahmā, a bit surprised.
No sound appears to fill his ears, no light to fill his eyes.

Unable to look down and see the basis of his throne,
Brahmā climbed down the stem and tried to find it on his own.
Just then he heard the syllables, '*ta pa*,' ring through the sky.
He thought, 'That stands for penance,' sat back down and closed his eyes.

A VISION OF THE KINGDOM OF GOD (45-51)

Brahmā did not see God but took His order through the ears,
and thus he sat in meditation for a thousand years.
Content with how sincerely Lord Brahmā had persevered,
Lord Vishṇu, and His world, Vaikuṇṭha, suddenly appeared.

Vaikuṇṭha's many citizens had skin of glowing blue,
with eyes like blooming lotuses and dress of golden hue.
Their youthful four-armed bodies, decked in gems and well-adorned,
appeared just like Lord Vishṇu in His bright, effulgent form.

Vaikuṇṭha's sky was full of planes that flew with flapping wing,
for in Vaikuṇṭha, consciousness infuses everything.
The beauty of the passengers was glittering and bright.
They dazzled Lord Brahmā like lightning flashing in the night.

He saw Śrī Laksmi, fortune's goddess, serve the Lord and sing,
as she and her companions wove an atmosphere of spring.
And then he saw the Lord Himself, with countless devotees,
in yellow robes and golden helmet, looking very pleased.

The Lord was seated on a throne and fully in command
of every cosmic energy. Brahmā could understand
the Lord was quite detached and unassuming in Himself
though full of beauty, wisdom, strength, celebrity and wealth.

The Lord looked at Brahmā, then shook his hand and slightly smiled.
'Your meditation pleased Me. I am ready now, My child,
to vest you with the power you'll require to create
the planets and all living things as I delineate.

I'm never pleased by mystic tricks of lofty platitudes,
but you've pleased Me by penance and your humble attitude.
This opportunity to see Me in My own domain
already passes all a meditator can attain.

THE *BHĀGAVAT*'S FOUR 'NUTSHELL VERSES' (52-55)

Before creation I was there, with nothing else but Me,
including lifeless matter, My less worthy energy.
As you fill up the universe, I'll witness your affairs,
and when it is annihilated, I shall still be there.

If something seems of value but is not attached to Me,
it surely is produced of My deceptive energy.
Do not desire such objects or invest them with affection.
They come not from the light of truth but from its dark reflection.

Components of creation, earth and water and the rest,
at once appear before us yet remain unmanifest.
I also live in everything, unseen by common eyes,
yet I exist outside it all, as you can realize.

In every circumstance, in every place and every time,
by personal experience or guesswork of the mind,
a seeker of the highest truth must come to know at last
that I am God in person and that I am unsurpassed.'

ŚAUNAKA'S REQUEST (56-62)

That said, the Personality of Godhead disappeared.
With folded hands, Brahmā began to fill the cosmic sphere
with planets, stars and bodies fit for every kind of being.
Lord Krishna thus directs Brahmā to fashion everything."

As Sūta then went on repeating Śukadeva's own words,
pertaining to creation and how each detail occurred,
sage Śaunaka stood up and asked to speak his heart's desire.
"Dear Sūta, there is something else of which I must inquire.

Before King Viṣṇurāta's deeds, which brought us to this stage,
you spoke about the travels of Vidura, the great sage.
You said he met Maitreya at a distant holy place.
Can you relate what happened when those two met face to face?"

While Sūta had described creation, it did not invoke
the sages' curiosity as much as when he spoke
directly of Lord Krishna. So, he shifted his narration
to Śukadeva's retelling of Maitreya's conversation.

Now Sūta will tell Śaunaka what Śukadeva said
about Maitreya's speech. Is that enough to spin your head?
"Now why," you well may ask, "when speakers rise to take the floor
do they just speak the Bhāgavat *as someone did before?"*

As lawyers cite authorities to sway the judge in court
and always quote a precedent to justify their tort,
so Krishna-talk has potency. Experience it yourself
by quoting from the Bhāgavat *to those you wish to help.*

[End of Second Canto of the *Bhāgavat Purāṇa*]

STRATEGY #12: TAKE ACTION

The previous section explains how a saint lets go of material attachments in preparation for death. Suppose we're ready for death yet the averages say we still have decades left to live. Where does that leave us?

It leaves us in a much better world.

Imagine for a moment a world of enlightened, saintly people. There would be no war, for no one would be unduly attached to material possessions, and everyone would see it in their best interest to forgive the transgressions of others. People would understand that all beings are spiritual souls and not discriminate against anyone on the basis of bodily considerations like race, gender, age, religion, ethnicity, or even species. Seeing all in relationship with the Supreme, they would have a sense of unity and brotherhood. And there would be no poverty, for everyone would choose a peaceful, simple life, taking only their minimal needs from the generous Earth. Even animals could live out their lives peacefully, giving their natural gifts for use by humans who would easily subsist on non-violent foods. Inhabited by such an enlightened human society, Mother Earth would recover her health and give abundantly for the safety and well-being of all her children.

Such an enlightened world requires enlightened people. Though challenging, enlightenment is easily within our grasp. Without demanding that we accept any religious dogma, bhakti-yoga easily leads us to enlightenment. But just knowing about it is not enough. If we want results, we have to take action.

Bhakti is a science which, if performed properly, yields the expected results every time. While the *Bhāgavat Purāṇa* describes the process of bhakti in detail, Sri Caitanya, the great exponent of the *Bhāgavat Purāṇa*, put it in a nutshell. He taught that, among other things, one seeking bhakti should:

- Practice meditation—not the difficult method of trying to artificially silence the mind, but the easy and effective method of reciting the names of God for extended periods, both to oneself and with others. Caitanya recited the names of Krishna (Hare Krishna Hare Krishna Krishna Krishna Hare Hare, Hare Rāma Hare Rāma Rāma Rāma Hare Hare). He also taught that any name of God would work in this powerful, non-sectarian practice.

- Read spiritual texts, especially the *Bhagavad-gītā* and *Bhāgavat Purāṇa*.

- Associate with spiritually minded people who are practicing the same spiritual techniques.

Without subscribing to any particular faith or philosophy, without paying a penny, an open-minded person can experiment with these simple techniques and see what happens. If one doesn't like the results, there is no risk, for bhakti comes with a karma-back guarantee—there is no contract, and we can always return to our previous lives.

By acting in bhakti we have nothing to lose and a more peaceful, fulfilling life to gain as we uncover the saint within.

AFTERWORD

The lotus flower, the Vedic emblem of beauty, is known as *pankaja*, a flower that rises from the mud. The lotus seed sprouts in the muck, reaches up through murky water and bursts into the air, blooming in gorgeous pink, blue or yellow tints.

Such is the life of a saint. Rising from any sort of background, pushing through uncertainty, the saint blossoms within the rarified air of pure human life. A saint may be unremarkable without, but within he or she brims with extraordinary qualities of love, compassion and wisdom.

The seed of saintliness lies within us all. One who takes up bhakti will find it simple to grow that seed. Yet, as the personalities described in this book show, life is less like a tranquil, lotus filled pond than a whitewater river. Life constantly rushes at us, challenging us to either set our own course or be pushed along by the persistent currents of a materialistic society.

Bhakti enables us to swim upstream in a river of materialism. The rewards of that challenging journey come not at the end but on the way, as we shed layers of bad habits and uncover our pure spiritual essence. Whatever else may be going on in the raging currents without, within themselves determined bhaktas continually bloom in increasing, holistic spiritual beauty.

If you accept the challenging course of real spiritual life, may your life and the lives of all who know you be blessed as your inner saint awakens.

Further reading on bhakti is available in the books listed on page 167.

-***Kd***

KEY PERSONALITIES

IN THE *BHĀGAVATA PURĀṆA* CANTOS ONE AND TWO

Abhimanyu – Arjuna's powerful and beloved son who was killed at Kurukṣetra. Husband of Uttarā and father of Viṣṇurāta.

Arjuna – The third of Pāṇḍu's five sons. An unparalleled archer, Arjuna was Droṇa's favorite student and Kṛṣṇa's beloved friend and student in the *Bhagavad-gītā*.

Aśvatthāmā – The noble Droṇa's son who became a terrorist.

Bali – The king of the *asuras* (demons) who reformed and surrendered to Kṛṣṇa. Grandfather of Prahlāda.

Bhīma – The second son of Pāṇḍu, known for superhuman strength.

Bhīṣma – The beloved uncle of Pāṇḍu, Vidura and Dhṛtarāṣṭra. A lifelong celibate, Bhīṣma was the elder statesman of the kingdom who, like Droṇa, was forced by Duryodhana to fight against the Pāṇḍavas. Duryodhana failed to heed Bhīṣma's good advice, resulting in disaster.

Brahmā – The chief demigod and first created being in each universe. Guided and empowered from within by Lord Kṛṣṇa, Brahmā in turn creates everything in the universe.

Devaki – Kṛṣṇa's mother.

Dharma – Morality, religiosity. Dharma personified appears as a bull in the *Bhāgavata*.

Dhṛtarāṣṭra – The aged, blind and indecisive king of the Kurus. Elder brother of the late King Pāṇḍu, nephew of Bhīṣma, husband of Gāndhārī. His sons, headed by Duryodhana, battled Pāṇḍu's sons.

Drupada – a king friendly to the Pāṇḍavas.

Draupadī – the daughter of Drupada who married all five Pāṇḍava brothers. She was attacked publicly by Duryodhana and his brothers. Aśvatthāmā killed her five sons.

Droṇa – The honorable military guru who taught the sons of both Pāṇḍu and Dhṛtarāṣṭra. By Duryodhana's manipulation Droṇa, against his will, was obliged to fight for his side. Father of Aśvatthāmā.

Duryodhana – Dhṛtarāṣṭra's eldest son and leader of the plots against the Pāṇḍavas.

Durvāsa – A powerful, sometimes irritable sage.

Gāndhārī – Wife of Dhṛtarāṣṭra, famed for her chastity.

Gāṇḍīva – Arjuna's celebrated bow, awarded to him by Agni.

Gopi – The cowherd maidens who loved Kṛṣṇa unconditionally.

Hiraṇyakaśipu – An ancient, powerful, devilish king who tortured his son Prahlāda and died at the hands of Nṛsiṁhadeva.

Jarāsandha – An enemy of Kṛṣṇa later killed by Bhīma.

Kali – in the Vedic calendar, the last of the four cyclical *yugas*, or ages. For the last 5000 years earth has been in the Kali age, and over 400,000 years remain. The Kali age is characterized by deceit, war and constant disturbances. Kali appears as a person in the *Bhāgavata*.

Kaṁsa – The evil king of Mathurā. He imprisoned Kṛṣṇā's parents Devakī and Vasudeva and was later killed by Kṛṣṇa.

Khaṭvāṅga – A king famed for remembering Kṛṣṇa at the moment of death.

Kṛpa – the elderly priest who fought against the Pāṇḍavas but later taught Viṣṇurāta.

Kṛṣṇa – The original Supreme Personality of Godhead, source of everyone and everything; the supreme controller, beneficiary and friend of everyone. In His personal pastimes, the cowherd boy, son of Nanda and Devakī who protects the inhabitants of Vṛndāvana, His home village. The original form of God and source of all other incarnations of God (avatars), full or partial.

Kuntī – Wife of Pāṇḍu and mother of the five Pāṇḍavas.

Lakṣmī – The goddess of fortune.

Maitreya – A renowned sage. His talks with Vidura form much of *Bhāgavata*'s Third Canto.

Maya – A mystic, devilish architect who built a meeting hall for the Pāṇḍavas. ('*Māyā*'refers to illusion.)

Nanda – Kṛṣṇa's foster father, king of the Vṛndāvana cowherdsmen.

Nārada – The ever-wandering eternal mystic, guru of Vyāsa and son of Brahmā.

Nārāyaṇa – A name of Lord Kṛṣṇa, usually referring to a Viṣṇu form.

Nṛsiṁhadeva – The ferocious half-man, half-lion incarnation of Kṛṣṇa.

Pāṇḍu – The righteous king and younger brother of Dhṛtarāṣṭra who inherited the worldwide kingdom based in Hastināpura. Father of the five Pāṇḍava brothers (Yudhiṣṭhira, Arjuna, Bhīma, Nakula and Sahadeva); husband of Kuntī and Mādri. A wise and popular monarch, he died before his sons were old enough to inherit his kingdom.

Prahlāda – Saintly son of Hiraṇyakaśipu and famed devotee of Nṛsiṁhadeva.

Rantideva – An ancient king cited as an example of generosity.

Sañjaya – Dhṛtarāṣṭra's faithful secretary and narrator of the *Bhagavad-gītā*.

Sarasvatī – The goddess of learning for whom a holy river in India is named.

Śaunaka – The sage chosen as spokesman for the assembly questioning Sūta.

Śibi – An ancient king cited as an example of self-sacrifice.

Śiva – One of the first sons of Brahmā; a partial incarnation of Kṛṣṇa charged with universal devastation. Though many worship Śiva as supreme, he is known as the greatest devotee of Kṛṣṇa.

Śṛīngi – A young brāhmaṇa who cursed King Viṣṇurāta to die.

Śukadeva – The secondary, yet principal speaker of the *Bhāgavata*. As the learned son of Vyāsa, Śukadeva was chosen to instruct King Viṣṇurāta when he was about to die.

Sūta – The primary speaker of the *Bhāgavata*. When consulted by an assembly of sages, Sūta answers many urgent questions presented by Śaunaka by recounting talks between Śukadeva and Viṣṇurāta.

Uttarā – The wife of Abhimanyu and mother of Viṣṇurāta.

Vasudeva – Kṛṣṇa's father and Devakī's husband.

Viṣṇu – The majestic, four-handed form of Kṛṣṇa; a nearly full incarnation of Kṛṣṇa worshipped by many.

Viṣṇurāta – The son of Arjuna's son Abhimanyu and his wife Uttarā. As the successor to Yudhiṣṭhira, he protected earth from Kali. He gave his life in deference to a brāhmaṇa's curse while hearing the *Bhāgavata* from Śukadeva. Also known as Pariksit Maharāja.

Vyāsa – A partial incarnation of Kṛṣṇa, famed as the compiler of the original Vedas and their supplements, including the *Mahābhārata*, the *Purāṇas* and the *Upaniṣads*.

Yadu – An ancient king who lent his name to the dynasty in which Kṛṣṇa appeared.

Yamarāja – The demigod charged with overseeing death and retribution for sins.

Yaśodā – Kṛṣṇa's adoptive mother in Vṛndāvana.

Yudhiṣṭhira – The eldest son of Pāṇḍu, known for complete honesty and righteousness, who gained his rightful kingdom after defeating Duryodhana at Kurukṣetra.

GLOSSARY

Bhāgavata – Pertaining to Kṛṣṇa, who is known as Bhagavān, the all-opulent one.

Brahmāstra – A mystic weapon of nuclear proportions, invoked by mantra and capable of either targeting an individual or creating mass destruction.

Dvārakā – Kṛṣṇa's capital city built off India's west coast.

Karma – Reactions to actions performed for material purposes. According to karma, one takes birth in a particular situation and enjoys and suffers through particular material experiences.

Kurukṣetra – Site of a massive war between the sons of Pāṇḍu and Dhṛtarāṣṭra; famed holy place near Delhi where *Bhagavad-gītā* was spoken.

Kuśa – A long grass cut and used as a sitting place for yogis.

Mathurā – The capital of the evil Kaṁsa located near Kṛṣṇa's village of Vṛndāvana.

Oṁ – A sound representation of the Supreme.

Purāṇas – Eighteen ancient Sanskrit texts written by Vyāsadeva to supplement the Vedas.

Śrī – Beautiful. Often used as a respectful form of address, such as "Śrī Kṛṣṇa".

Supersoul (In Sanskrit, *paramātmā*) – Kṛṣṇa's incarnation in the heart of everyone and everything.

Vaikuṇṭha – Literally "without anxiety"; the spiritual abode of Viṣṇu.

Vaiṣṇava – A devotee of Viṣṇu or Kṛṣṇa.

Varṇāśrama – The social system that identifies people by *varṇa*, natural work inclination, and *āśrama*, progressive spiritual status. The four *varṇas* are:

Brāhmaṇa (priests, teachers, intellectuals, judges)
Kṣatriya (warriors, administrators)
Vaiśya (entrepreneurs, merchants)
Śūdra (workers, artisans, assistants for others)

The four *āśramas* include:

Brahmacārī (celibate student life)
Gṛhastha (spiritual married life)
Vānaprastha (retired, spiritually focused life)
Sannyāsa (fully renounced life)

Vedas – The extensive body of Sanskrit literature covering a wide variety of spiritual and physical subjects. Veda means knowledge. The original four Vedas include the *Ṛg*, *Atharva*, *Sāma* and *Yajur*. Supplementary Vedic literatures include the *Purāṇas*, *Upaniṣads*, *Mahābhārata*, *Rāmāyaṇa*, and many others. *Bhagavad-gītā* is popularly known as the quintessential text of Vedic philosophy.

Vraja – The greater district of Vṛndāvana.

Vṛndāvana – Kṛṣṇā's beloved home village. Today a famous holy place near Delhi.

Yoga – Linking with God. The *Bhagavad-gītā* discusses many varieties of yoga, culminating with bhakti-yoga, or union with God through loving devotional service.

FOR FURTHER READING

Books by Śrila A.C. Bhaktivedānta Swami Prabhupāda:

- *Bhagavad-Gītā As It Is*
- *Śrī Īśopaniṣad*
- *Śrīmad-Bhāgavatam*
- *Caitanya-caritāmṛta*
- *The Nectar of Instruction*
- *The Nectar of Devotion*

Books by Other Authors:

- *Bhagavad gītā: The Beloved Lord's Secret Love Song*, by Dr. Graham Schweig
- *Dance of Divine Love*, by Dr. Graham Schweig
- *Surrender Unto Me*, by Bhurijan Das
- *A Comprehensive Guide to Bhagavad-Gītā with Literal Translation*, by H.D. Goswami

Other books by Kalakaṇṭha Das:

- *A God Who Dances*
- *Bhagavad-Gītā: The Rap of God*
- *All That Lies Between*

ACKNOWLEDGEMENTS

Editing & Content Advice:

Lavana Mangala Devi, Prabhupada Priya Devi, Syamali Devi

General Advice:

Hridayananda Goswami, Satsvarupa Goswami,
Krishna Kripa Dāsa, Keshihanta Dāsa

Publication Assistance:

Radha Jivan Dāsa

Layout & Cover Design:

Bhīṣmadeva Dāsa / HoofprintMedia.com